THE FREE SEA

NATURAL LAW AND
ENLIGHTENMENT CLASSICS

Knud Haakonssen
General Editor

Hugo Grotius

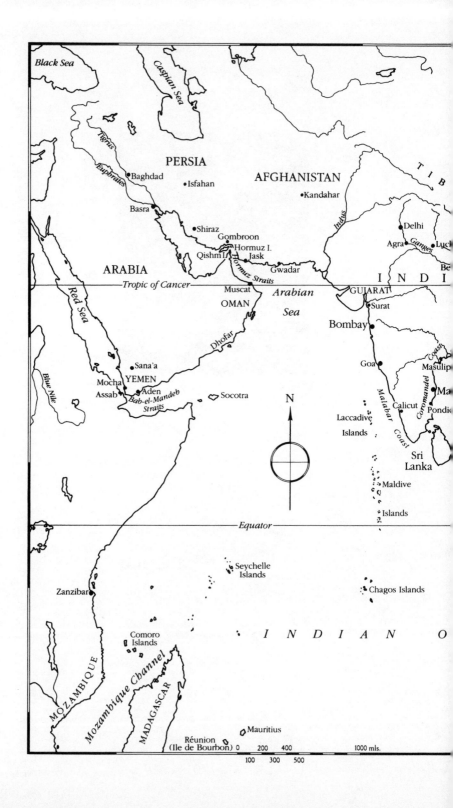

Black Sea

Caspian Sea

Tigris

Euphrates

PERSIA

•Baghdad

•Isfahan

AFGHANISTAN

•Kandahar

Basra

•Shiraz

Gombroon

Hormuz I.

Qishm I.

Jask

Indus

TIB

Delhi

Agra

Ganges

Luck

Be

ARABIA

Tropic of Cancer

Gwadar

Muscat

Hormuz Straits

I N D I

GUIARAT

Surat

Arabian

Sea

OMAN

Red Sea

Dhofar

Bombay

Goa

Masulip

Coast

Blue Nile

•Sana'a

YEMEN

Mocha

Assab

Aden

Bab-el-Mandeb
Straits

Socotra

N

Malabar Coast

Coromandel

Calicut

Ma

Pondic

Laccadive

Islands

Sri
Lanka

Maldive

Islands

Equator

Seychelle
Islands

Zanzibar

Chagos Islands

I N D I A N   O

Comoro
Islands

MOZAMBIQUE

Mozambique Channel

MADAGASCAR

Réunion
(Ile de Bourbon)

Mauritius

0   200   400   1000 mls.

100   300   500

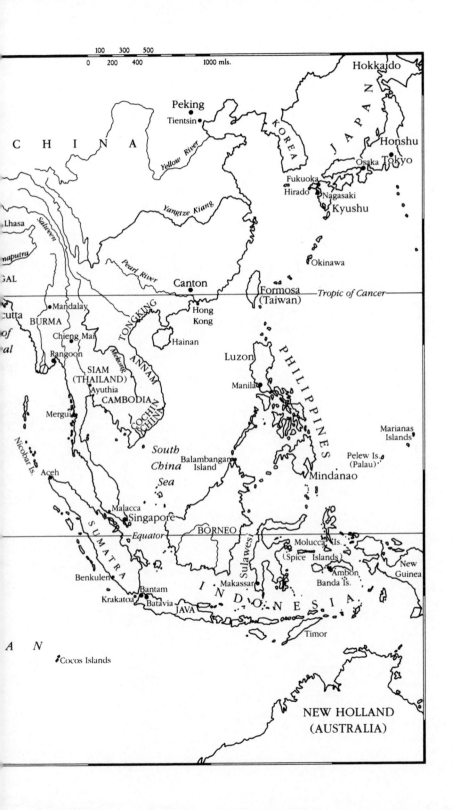

100 300 500

0 200 400 1000 mls.

CHINA

Lhasa

Salween

Brahmaputra

BENGAL

Calcutta

of

Bengal

BURMA

Mandalay

Chieng Mai

Rangoon

Mergui

Nicobar Is.

Aceh

SIAM
(THAILAND)

Ayuthia

CAMBODIA

COCHIN
CHINA

ANNAM

TONGKING

Mekong

Yellow River

Yangtze Kiang

Pearl River

Peking

Tientsin

Canton

Hong
Kong

Hainan

South
China
Sea

Malacca

Singapore

SUMATRA

Benkulen

Krakatoa

Bantam

Batavia

JAVA

Equator

BORNEO

INDONESIA

Sulawesi

Makassar

Balambangan
Island

Luzon

Manila

PHILIPPINES

Mindanao

Formosa
(Taiwan)

Tropic of Cancer

Okinawa

KOREA

JAPAN

Hokkaido

Honshu

Osaka Tokyo

Fukuoka

Hirado Nagasaki

Kyushu

Marianas
Islands

Pelew Is.
(Palau)

Molucca Is.
(Spice Islands)

Ambon

Banda Is.

New
Guinea

Timor

OCEAN

Cocos Islands

NEW HOLLAND
(AUSTRALIA)

NATURAL LAW AND
ENLIGHTENMENT CLASSICS

The Free Sea

Hugo Grotius

Translated by Richard Hakluyt

with William Welwod's Critique
and Grotius's Reply

Edited and with an Introduction
by David Armitage

Major Legal and Political Works of Hugo Grotius

LIBERTY FUND

This book is published by Liberty Fund, Inc., a foundation established
to encourage study of the ideal of a society of free and responsible individuals.

𒂼𒄄

The cuneiform inscription that serves as our logo and as the design motif for
our endpapers is the earliest-known written appearance of the word
"freedom" (*amagi*), or "liberty." It is taken from a clay document written
about 2300 B.C. in the Sumerian city-state of Lagash.

04 19 20 21 22   C   5   4   3   2   1
19 20 21 22 23   P   8   7   6   5   4

Frontispiece: Portrait of Hugo de Groot by Michiel van Mierevelt, 1608;
oil on panel; collection of Historical Museum Rotterdam, on loan from the
Van der Mandele Stichting. Reproduced by permission.

Map of the Far East on pp. iv–v reproduced from John Keay,
The Honourable Company: A History of the East India Company,
published by Harper Collins, London: 1990. Used by permission.

Library of Congress Cataloging-in-Publication Data
Grotius, Hugo, 1583–1645.
[Mare liberum. English]
The free sea / Hugo Grotius;
translated by Richard Hakluyt with William Welwod's critique and Grotius's reply;
edited and with an introduction by David Armitage.
p. cm.—(Natural law and enlightenment classics)
"The major legal and political works of Hugo Grotius."
Includes bibliographical references and index.
ISBN 0-86597-430-6 (hbk.: alk. paper)—ISBN 0-86597-431-4 (pbk.: alk. paper)
1. Freedom of the seas. I. Hakluyt, Richard, 1552?–1616.
II. Welwod, William, fl. 1578–1622.
III. Armitage, David, 1965– IV. Title. V. Series.
KZA1348.G7613 2004
343.09'6—dc22   2003060575

LIBERTY FUND, INC.
11301 North Meridian Street
Carmel, Indiana 46032

CONTENTS

INTRODUCTION

Few works of such brevity can have caused arguments of such global extent and striking longevity as Hugo Grotius's *Mare Liberum* (*The Free Sea*). The book first appeared in Leiden as a pocket-sized quarto volume from the famous publishing house of Elzevier in the spring of 1609. The publication was anonymous, perhaps because (as Grotius later wrote) "it seemed to me to be safe, like a painter skulking behind his easel, to find out the judgment of others and to consider more carefully anything that might be published to the contrary" (*Defense*, p. 78, below). Grotius was only in his late twenties but already possessed a reputation as one of Europe's most precocious and penetrating humanist scholars. Though self-taught as a lawyer, his reputation as an advocate and adviser was growing, along with his political influence. By publishing *Mare Liberum,* he was displaying the literary, rhetorical, and philosophical talents that had won him his burgeoning fame and respect, and he was also intervening in two political debates of pivotal significance for his own country. The first was the relationship between the United Provinces and the Spanish monarchy, from which the Dutch had broken away in 1581; the second was the Dutch right to commercial penetration in Southeast Asia. Although the arena of dispute was local, the implications of *Mare Liberum's* arguments were global. The book was taken by the English and the Scots as an assault on their fishing rights in the North Sea and by the Spanish as an attack on the foundations of their overseas empire. It had implications no less for coastal waters than it did for the high seas, for the West Indies as much as for the East Indies, and for intra-European disputes as well as for relations between the European powers and extra-European peoples.

The immediate context for the publication of *Mare Liberum* was the process of negotiating a truce between the Dutch and the Spanish to end the decades of contention that had begun with the Dutch revolt of the late sixteenth century.[1] Among the issues on the table during these discussions was the question of Dutch access to the expanding markets of the East Indies, where the Dutch were engaged in cut-throat competition with the Portuguese, the Spanish, and, increasingly, the English for the huge profits to be gained from trade in silks, spices, porcelain, and other luxury goods. This was, of course, no novel dispute in 1609, but the process of drawing up a definitive truce between the Dutch and the Spanish had brought matters to a head, not least for the Dutch East India Company (VOC). Indeed, it was at the insistence of the Zeeland Chamber of the VOC in the autumn of 1608 that Grotius prepared *Mare Liberum* for publication, just as it had been at the VOC's behest that he had originally written it as part of a larger work in 1604.[2]

The original occasion for the composition of the text that would later comprise *Mare Liberum* had been the major international dispute occasioned by the Dutch seizure of a Portuguese vessel in the Straits of Singapore in February 1603.[3] On that occasion, the Dutch captain Jakob van Heemskerck had captured the carrack *Sta. Catarina*, which was carrying a fabulously wealthy cargo of trade goods. When its contents were sold in Amsterdam, they grossed more than three million guilders, a sum equivalent to just less than the annual revenue of the English government at the time and more than double the capital of the English East India Company.[4] A prize of such magnitude generated an equally prominent debate

1. Martine van Ittersum, "Profit and Principle: Hugo Grotius, Natural Rights Theories and the Rise of Dutch Power in the East Indies, 1595–1615" (Ph.D. dissertation, Harvard University, 2002), 442–53.

2. For correspondence from November 1608 to [April] 1609 relating to the publication of *Mare Liberum*, see *Briefwisseling van Hugo Grotius*, ed. P. C. Molhuysen, B. L. Meulenbroek, and H. J. M. Nellen, 17 vols. (The Hague: M. Nijhoff, 1928–2001), I, 128–34, 139–41, 144–45.

3. Peter Borschberg, "The Seizure of the *Sta. Catarina* Revisited: The Portuguese Empire in Asia, VOC Politics and the Origins of the Dutch-Johor Alliance (1602–ca. 1616)," *Journal of Southeast Asian Studies* 33 (2002): 31–62.

4. Richard Tuck, *The Rights of War and Peace: Political Thought and the International Order from Grotius to Kant* (Oxford: Oxford University Press, 1999), 80; Borschberg, "The Seizure of the *Sta. Catarina* Revisited": 35.

about the legitimacy of the Dutch capture of a Portuguese vessel in the distant seas of the East Indies. The twenty-one-year-old Grotius was drafted to supply a defense of the VOC's position that the ship had been taken as booty in a just war: As he recalled later, "The universal laws of war and prize (*universi belli praedaeque jura*), and the story of the dire and cruel deeds perpetrated by the Portuguese upon our fellow-countrymen, and many other things pertaining to this subject, I treated in a rather long *Commentary* which up to the present I have refrained from publishing" (*Defense,* p. 77, below). The manuscript of that commentary remained unknown to posterity until it resurfaced at a sale of de Groot family papers in 1864. Its discovery revealed that *Mare Liberum* was substantially identical to the twelfth chapter of the work usually referred to by Grotius himself as *De rebus Indicis* (*On the Affairs of the Indies*),[5] though better known by the title given to it by its first editor, *De Jure Praedae Commentarius* (*Commentary on the Law of Prize and Booty*).[6]

Although *Mare Liberum's* influence and importance were—and remain—independent of that larger commentary, they cannot be fully understood outside of the argument of which they formed a part. Grotius defended the Dutch seizure of the *Sta. Catarina* on the basis of a set of natural laws, which he derived originally from the divine will.[7] The two primary laws of nature were self-defense and self-preservation. He defined self-preservation as acquiring and retaining anything useful for life, a process which assumed that God had bestowed the gifts of his creation upon all human beings collectively but on none particularly: Only through physical seizure (*possessio*) leading to use (*usus*) could ownership (*dominium*) be derived. Two further laws, of inoffensiveness (harm no one) and abstinence (do not seize the possessions of others), set limits to these pri-

5. For example, *Briefwisseling van Hugo Grotius,* ed. Molhuysen, Meulenbroek, and Nellen, I, 72 ("de rebus Indicis opusculum").

6. Hugo Grotius, *De Jure Praedae Commentarius,* ed. H. G. Hamaker (The Hague: M. Nijhoff, 1868); Grotius, *De Jure Praedae Commentarius,* 2 vols. (Oxford: Oxford University Press, 1950). All references in the text are to the translation in the first volume of the latter edition.

7. Richard Tuck, *Philosophy and Government, 1572–1651* (Cambridge: Cambridge University Press, 1993), 169–79.

mary laws; from these followed two further laws of justice: that evil deeds should be punished and that good deeds should be rewarded (*De Jure Praedae*, pp. 8, 10, 11, 13, 15). Together, these laws provided the basis for Grotius's judgment of the facts of Luso-Dutch relations in the East Indies. If it could be shown that the Portuguese had committed evil deeds against the Dutch and against their indigenous allies, and if it could be shown that van Heemskerck had engaged in a just war against the Portuguese captain of the *Sta. Catarina,* then his spoils taken in that war would be a legitimate prize for the corporate body on whose behalf he acted, the VOC itself.

The bulk of Grotius's argument turned on the two issues of law and fact. In the first third of *De Jure Praedae,* he laid out the conditions under which booty might be justly seized by Christians from other Christians and the broader circumstances that defined a war between Christians as just. Having established the terms of law, he turned to matters of fact in a detailed narrative of relations since the Dutch revolt between the Dutch on one side and the Spanish and Portuguese on the other, to show that "[t]he latter . . . have invariably set an example of perfidy and cruelty; the Dutch, an example of clemency and good faith" (*De Jure Praedae,* p. 171). Then, in the twelfth chapter of his defense, Grotius went on to argue "that even if the war were a private war, it would be just, and the prize would be justly acquired by the Dutch East India Company" (*De Jure Praedae,* p. 216).

When Grotius came to publish that chapter as *Mare Liberum,* he made no reference to the case of the *Sta. Catarina* or to the supposed facts of Portuguese aggression and depredation in the East Indies. Instead, he prefaced his argument with a refutation of skepticism about the natural basis of moral distinctions (*The Free Sea,* pp. 5–6, below). Against the instrumentalist view that such distinctions had been invented solely to benefit the powerful in their rule over the powerless, Grotius affirmed that the laws of nature are the product of divine will and that they can be universally understood by the application of natural reason. He again argued that God had created the world in common for all humanity but that property could be acquired through human "labor and industry," subject to two of the primary natural laws he had set down in *De Jure Praedae:* "that all surely might use common things without the damage of all and, for the rest, every man contented with his portion shall abstain from another's" (*The Free Sea,* p. 6, below).

Freedom of navigation and trade (*commeandi commercandique libertas*) exemplified those principles, whether applied to particular communities or to the universal society of humanity. To support this contention, Grotius appealed to Greek and Roman literature, to Roman law (in particular, to *Institutes,* II. I. I and *Digest,* I. 8. 4), and to sixteenth-century Spanish authorities, above all the Dominican theologian Francisco de Vitoria and his fellow Salamancan, the jurist Fernando Vázquez de Menchaca. A notable omission from his battery of authorities was Scripture, a resource that Grotius's Scottish antagonist, William Welwod, would later exploit. However, by framing his argument in this way, Grotius could illustrate the obligations of natural (rather than revealed) religion, beyond the interpretive traditions of particular denominations, and show that even the juristic traditions of the Spanish monarchy (which since 1580 had included Portugal) opposed the Portuguese. His broader framing of the argument also ensured that *Mare Liberum* would be understood as a general statement of the right to freedom of trade and navigation. In this way, it sparked a wider and more enduring controversy regarding the foundations of international relations, the limits of national sovereignty, and the relationship between sovereignty (*imperium*) and possession (*dominium*) that would guarantee its lasting fame and notoriety.

Grotius broke down the Portuguese claim of exclusive access to the East Indies into three constituent parts: the right of possession, the right of navigation, and the right of trade. The Portuguese could claim no right of possession by virtue of first discovery, because the lands of the East Indies were not *terra nullius* (unpossessed land) but were in the possession of their native rulers. The fact that those rulers were "partly idolaters, partly Mahometans" did not invalidate their right to dominion (*The Free Sea,* p. 14, below): As Aquinas and Vitoria had argued (against earlier thinkers like Hostiensis and John Wycliffe), grace could not confer dominion. Nor were the peoples of Southeast Asia "out of their wits and insensible but ingenious and sharp-witted." No assumptions of tutelage, or even appeals to Aristotelian conceptions of natural servitude, could therefore be employed to dispossess them, as Vitoria had likewise argued against the use of such arguments in the Americas (*The Free Sea*, p. 15, below). Papal donation could not have transferred *dominium* to the Portuguese because the pope possessed no temporal power, least of all over infidels (as, yet again, Vitoria had argued in relation to the New World). The only possible remaining claim was by "right of prey" (*jure praedae*) or conquest; however, that too was inapplicable to the Portuguese case, because the indigenous peoples had supplied no *casus belli* on which a claim to conquest in a just war could have been founded. With this reprise of four centuries of European arguments regarding the dispossession of the "barbarian," Grotius left the Portuguese with no legitimate argument for possession. He then turned to their arguments for exclusive navigation and commerce.

Only at this point did Grotius directly address the subject of his title (*Mare Liberum, The Free Sea*) rather than his subtitle (*De Jure quod Batavis Competit ad Indicana Commercio, The Right Which the Hollanders Ought to Have to the Indian Merchandise for Trading*), as his argument shifted from rights over land to those over the sea. This distinction between territorial and maritime possession rested on a yet more fundamental difference between those things that could be appropriated and those that remained common by nature. If (as Grotius had argued in the body of *De Jure Praedae*) *dominium* could be derived only from use based on physical apprehension (*possessio*), only those things capable both of possession and of use could be appropriated from their pristine state of natural community, subject to the proviso that no other person should be harmed by the act of appropriation (an important limiting factor that permitted the private appropriation of the seashore but not at the expense of common access or use). On these grounds, Grotius argued that neither the Portuguese nor anyone else could claim exclusive possession of the ocean around and leading to the East Indies. Because the sea is fluid and ever changing, it cannot be possessed; because it (and its resources, such as fish) is apparently inexhaustible, it cannot be used: "[t]he sea therefore is in the number of things which are not in merchandise and trading, that is to say, cannot remain proper" (*The Free Sea*, p. 30, below). The land, by contrast, can be physically circumscribed, human labor does transform it, and its products are rendered private by their use. This fundamental contrast between the

properties of sea and land would remain central to later conceptions of
property within the natural-law tradition up to and beyond John Locke's
agriculturalist argument for appropriation, which similarly exempted "the
Ocean, that great and still remaining Common of Mankind" (Locke, *Second Treatise*, § 30) from the possibility of exclusive possession.[8]

· Yet if the Portuguese could claim no right of possession (*dominium*)
over the sea, the question remained whether they could still claim jurisdiction (*imperium*), which would allow them to debar others from trade
with the East Indies. In the last part of the work, Grotius rebutted Portuguese claims to exclusive rights of trade. He argued that the right of navigation could not be appropriated by the Portuguese or anyone else (in-
cluding the pope). Because that right of navigation was an objective
feature of natural law, it could not be altered by human custom or by prescription, as Grotius showed with extensive quotations from Vázquez de
Menchaca (a proponent of the freedom of the seas, to be sure, but also an
exponent of the idea that navigation was not only unnatural but also sui-
cidally dangerous, a feature of Vázquez's argument Grotius conveniently
ignored).[9] As with the right of navigation, so with the right of trading,
which was also "agreeable to the primary law of nations" (*The Free Sea*,
p. 51, below). After this point, Grotius added a new conclusion to the material he had drawn from *De Jure Praedae*, arguing that "we wholly maintain that liberty which we have by nature, whether we have peace, truce or
war with the Spaniard," but with the threat attached that "he that shall
stop the passage and hinder the carrying out of merchandise may be resisted by way of fact, as they say, even without expecting any public authority" (*The Free Sea*, p. 60, below).

The Twelve Years' Truce between the Dutch republic and the Spanish
monarchy was soon ratified, but *Mare Liberum*'s relevance was not dimin-

---

8. John Locke, *Two Treatises of Government*, ed. Peter Laslett (Cambridge: Cambridge University Press, 1988), 289. Locke possessed Grotius, *"De mari libero,"* in his
copy of the 1680 Hague edition of *De Jure Belli ac Pacis:* John Harrison and Peter Laslett, *The Library of John Locke* (Oxford: Oxford University Press, 1965), item 1331.

9. Fernando Vázquez de Menchaca, *Controversiarum illustrium . . . libri tres* (Frankfurt, 1572), II. 20. 11–20.

ished. Grotius's arguments could still justify the VOC's encroachment on the Portuguese colonial empire, despite the armistice in Europe; and their applicability to other contemporary disputes regarding the freedom of navigation, trade, and fishing made *Mare Liberum* a shot heard around the world. Its rebuttal of papal claims ensured that it was rapidly placed on the Church's *Index* of prohibited books in January 1610.[10] Sophisticated and extensive responses also came from the jurists William Welwod in Scotland (*An Abridgement of All Sea-Lawes* [1613]; *De Dominio Maris* [1615]), John Selden in England (*Mare Clausum* [ca. 1618]), Justo Seraphim de Freitas in Portugal (*De Justo Imperio Lusitanorum Asiatico* [1625]), and Juan Solórzano Pereira in Spain (*De Indiarum Jure* [1629]).

The only response to which Grotius replied was Welwod's *Abridgement.* Grotius had been shown Welwod's book in 1613, when he was in London as a delegate to the Anglo-Dutch colonial conference, and he took it to be *"exemplar Servi Maris"* ("the pattern of the unfree sea").[11] Welwod had understood *Mare Liberum*'s alleged East Indian context as a cover for the work's real purpose: to reinforce the claims of the Dutch herring-fleets to fish in British (in particular, Scottish) territorial waters. Those claims were indeed a topic of much contention after 1610, and Welwod could be forgiven for suspecting *Mare Liberum*'s contingent applicability. Yet Welwod stressed only the argument about fishing, ignored the broader questions of trade and navigation, and concentrated his fire on the fifth chapter of *Mare Liberum* alone. Like Grotius, he argued from the precedents of Roman law, but he also appealed to Scripture to argue that the sea could be occupied and hence acquired as the basis for customary claims to exclusive national rights over territorial waters. However, Welwod excepted the high seas from such claims to exclusive possession and agreed with Grotius that they should remain *"mare vastum liberrimum"* ("the great and most free sea": Welwod, "Of the Community and Propriety of the Seas," p. 74, below). That major concession was not enough to secure Grotius's assent to

10. Franz Heinrich Reusch, *Der Index der verbotenen Bücher,* 2 vols. (Bonn: M. Cohen and Son, 1883–85), II, 102.

11. J. Boreel to Hugo Grotius, 5 May 1614 (N.S.), *Briefwisseling van Hugo Grotius,* ed. Molhuysen, Meulenbroek, and Nellen, XVII, 111.

Welwod's arguments, to which he replied at length in the unpublished *Defensio capitis quinti Maris Liberi (Defense of the Fifth Chapter of "Mare Liberum")* (ca. 1615).[12]

In the *Defense of . . . "Mare Liberum,"* Grotius insisted even more firmly that land and sea were incommensurable because the one can be appropriated and the other cannot. He had to do so not least to refute Welwod's scriptural argument that God had given both earth and sea to humanity in common, an assertion that encouraged Grotius to reinforce the distinction between particular appropriation and universal possession, and hence between those things that are (or can become) private and those that remain in common. He even went further than he had needed (or dared) in *Mare Liberum* to argue that necessity—in the case of famine, for example—could render "common again things formerly owned" (*Defense*, p. 86, below). To clarify his definition of community, Grotius had to distinguish it from anything public (that is, owned by a particular nation or people) on the grounds that community of property was natural, whereas anything public was civil and hence the product of human will. From this, it was but a short step to two crucial moves that would characterize his political theory in *De Jure Belli ac Pacis:* first, his argument that the freedom of the seas derived not only from nature but also from custom and hence from consent (an anticipation of his later theory of property: *De Jure Belli ac Pacis,* II. 2. 2, § 5); and, second, that the right (*jus*) to trade or navigation was legitimate not by virtue of being a norm of objective justice but because it was "a moral faculty over a thing" (*Defense*, p. 107, below) (an anticipation of his highly influential theory of rights as subjective moral qualities: *De Jure Belli ac Pacis,* I. 1. 4).[13]

---

12. Hugo Grotius, "Defensio capitis quinti Maris Liberi oppugnati a Guilielmo Welwodo . . . capite XXVII ejus libri . . . cui titulum fecit Compendium Legum Maritimarum" (ca. 1615), in Samuel Muller, *Mare Clausum: Bijdrage tot de Geschiedenis der Rivaliteit van Engeland en Nederland in de Zeventiende Eeuw* (Amsterdam: F. Muller, 1872), 331–61. This must be the "geschrift de Piscatura" ("the tract *On Fishing*") referred to by Grotius in 1622: Grotius to Nicolaes van Reigersberch, 14 April 1622 (O.S.), *Briefwisseling van Hugo Grotius,* ed. Molhuysen, Meulenbroek, and Nellen, II, 204.

13. Knud Haakonssen, "Hugo Grotius and the History of Political Thought," *Political Theory* 13 (1985): 240, 242–43.

The *Defense,* like *Mare Liberum,* marked a crucial stage in the development of Grotius's mature political theory. The argument of *Mare Liberum* had already come back to haunt him when, as a negotiator for the Dutch in fishing disputes with the English in 1613, he justified English exclusion from Dutch fishing grounds. In ignorance of the identity of the work's author, the English envoys threw back the arguments of the *"assertor Maris liberi"* (the defender of the free sea) in Grotius's own face.[14] Even this discomfiting incident may have had a place in Grotius's philosophical development, as it caused him to refine the limits of his theory of property while he traveled the road toward *De Jure Belli ac Pacis.* Indeed, by 1625 he had come to agree with Welwod that territorial waters could be possessed (*De Jure Belli ac Pacis,* II. 3. 13–15). Yet the significance of *Mare Liberum* was not confined to the progress of Grotius's own thought: The classic dispute between *mare liberum* and *mare clausum* (represented most famously by Selden's "deeply Grotian" reply to Grotius)[15] lasted for much of the seventeenth century, flared up intermittently in the eighteenth and nineteenth, and was decided only in the twentieth.[16] Anyone wanting an accessible introduction to that epochal argument, to the genesis of modern theories of property and sovereignty, or to Grotius's political theory could do no better than begin with his compact classic, *Mare Liberum.*

David Armitage

14. English Commissioners to Dutch Commissioners, 9 May 1613 (O.S.), in G. N. Clark and W. J. M. van Eysinga, *The Colonial Conferences Between England and the Netherlands in 1613 and 1615, Bibliotheca Visseriana* 15 (1940), 116.

15. Tuck, *Philosophy and Government, 1572–1651,* 213.

16. Thomas Wemyss Fulton, *The Sovereignty of the Sea* (London: W. Blackwood, 1911).

A NOTE ON THE TEXTS

Hugo Grotius, *The Free Sea,* trans. Richard Hakluyt

There have been only two English translations of *Mare Liberum.* The last was in 1916, as part of the series of classics in the history of international law published by the Carnegie Endowment for International Peace.[1] This translation was avowedly a product of debates on neutral shipping during the First World War: "Since the month of August, 1914, the expression 'Freedom of the Seas' has been on the lips of belligerent and neutral, and it seems as advisable as it is timely to issue—for the first time in English— the famous Latin tractate of Grotius proclaiming, explaining, and in no small measure making the 'freedom of the seas.'"[2] However, though the Carnegie Endowment's edition may have been the first translation "issue[d]" in English, it was not the only, or even the first, English translation. That had been undertaken three hundred years before by the great English memorialist of overseas activity and promoter of English trade and colonization Richard Hakluyt the younger.[3]

The manuscript of the translation in the Inner Temple Library in London (MS Petyt 529) is a fair copy in Hakluyt's own hand. The twenty-six-leaf quarto was originally bound in vellum, of which a small patch survives

1. Hugo Grotius, *The Freedom of the Seas,* trans. Ralph Van Deman Magoffin (New York: Oxford University Press, American Branch, 1916).

2. James Brown Scott, "Introductory Note," in Grotius, *The Freedom of the Seas,* trans. Magoffin, p. v. The first German translation followed in 1919: Grotius, *Von der Freiheit des Meeres,* ed. and trans. Richard Boschan (Leipzig: F. Meiner, 1919).

3. George Bruner Parks, *Richard Hakluyt and the English Voyages* (New York: American Geographical Society, 1928), 212–13, 257; D. B. Quinn and A. M. Quinn, "A Hakluyt Chronology," in *The Hakluyt Handbook,* ed. D. B. Quinn, 2 vols. (London: Hakluyt Society, 1974), I, 324.

containing the title "Mare liberum / The free Sea." The flyleaf notes that it was "Translated into English by Mr Rich: Hackluyt &c."[4] Only brief extracts from the translation have ever been printed.[5] It has attracted little commentary from Hakluyt scholars and remains entirely unknown to scholars of Grotius, let alone to any wider readership. This edition therefore represents the first publication of an unknown contemporary translation of a major work in the history of political thought by a translator of historical significance in his own right.

The Free Sea was one of only three book-length translations Hakluyt himself undertook. The two others—from the French and Portuguese—both appeared in print during Hakluyt's lifetime.[6] The only translation from the Latin—of a linguistic manual for European travelers to the East Indies—with which his name has been associated was commissioned by the English East India Company in 1614.[7] It is unclear whether Hakluyt was responsible for the translation or was simply the agent by which it reached the company.[8] It is nonetheless possible that The Free Sea was the result of a commission from the company. The arguments of The Free Sea could just as easily have supported the English company's claims against the Portuguese as the VOC's and were, moreover, used during the Anglo-Dutch colonial conferences of 1613 and 1615 to combat Dutch pretensions to exclusive access to the East Indies. However, no payments to Hakluyt for a translation are recorded in the Court Books of the East India Company. Until further evidence is discovered, the occasion for his translation and the reason it was not published can only be matters for speculation. All that is certain is that the translation can have been undertaken no ear-

4. Hugo Grotius, "The Free Sea," trans. Richard Hakluyt, Inner Temple Library, MS Petyt 529, fol. 2r.

5. The Original Writings and Correspondence of the Two Richard Hakluyts, ed. E. G. R. Taylor, 2 vols. (London: Hakluyt Society, 1935), II, 497–99.

6. F. M. Rogers, "Hakluyt as Translator," in The Hakluyt Handbook, ed. Quinn, I, 37–39.

7. Gotthard Arthus, Dialogues in the English and Malaiane Languages, trans. Augustine Spalding (London, 1614).

8. Quinn and Quinn, "A Hakluyt Chronology," in The Hakluyt Handbook, ed. Quinn, I, 328; Calendar of State Papers, Colonial Series, ed. W. Nöel Sainsbury et al., 40 vols. (London: Great Britain Public Record Office, 1860–1926), II: East Indies, China and Japan, 1513–1616, 272.

lier than the publication of *Mare Liberum* in the spring of 1609 and no later than Hakluyt's death in November 1616.

It has been said that Hakluyt "stood very high in the two aspects of translation concerning which modern readers are most demanding. The one is mastery of technical vocabulary; the other is unraveling of complicated syntax."[9] Neither of these qualities is conspicuous in his translation of *The Free Sea*. Hakluyt's occasional mistranslations reveal his ignorance of the technical vocabulary of the law, particularly Roman law; Grotius's original Latin has been included as necessary in the footnotes to clarify these mistranslations. Hakluyt's translation is also quite literal in its adherence to Grotius's Latin syntax; to clarify the meaning of the text, spelling and punctuation have been modernized throughout.

The Inner Temple manuscript is a fair copy but contains a few minor emendations by Hakluyt himself; these have been silently incorporated into the text. The manuscript does not include Grotius's marginal annotations; these have been supplied from the 1609 text of *Mare Liberum* and have been expanded, supplemented, and corrected as necessary.

Editorial additions to the text are indicated by square brackets.

William Welwod, "Of the Community and Propriety of the Seas" (1613)

William Welwod was professor of mathematics and of civil law at the University of St. Andrews in Scotland and produced the first British treatise on the law of the sea, in 1590.[10] His reply to Chapter V of *Mare Liberum* comprised Chapter XXVII of his next work on maritime law, *An Abridgement of All Sea-Lawes* (1613).[11] Two years later, he expanded his criticisms of Grotius at the behest of Anne of Denmark, the wife of King James VI and I, in his *De dominio maris* (1615).[12] The text printed here is a modern-

9. Rogers, "Hakluyt as Translator," in *The Hakluyt Handbook,* ed. Quinn, I, 45.

10. William Welwod, *The Sea Law of Scotland* (Edinburgh, 1590).

11. William Welwod, *An Abridgement of All Sea-Lawes* (London, 1613), 61–72.

12. William Welwod, *De dominio maris* (London, 1615); J. D. Alsop, "William Welwod, Anne of Denmark and the Sovereignty of the Sea," *Scottish Historical Review* 49 (1980): 171–74.

ized version of Chapter XXVII of Welwod's *Abridgement,* with Welwod's marginal references expanded and amended to follow current practices for citing classical, biblical, and Roman law texts.

Hugo Grotius, "Defense of Chapter V of the *Mare Liberum*" (ca. 1615), trans. Herbert F. Wright

The manuscript of Grotius's reply to Welwod, like that of *De Jure Praedae,* was discovered in 1864 among the de Groot family papers.[13] Entitled the "Defensio capitis quinti Maris Liberi oppugnati a Guilielmo Welwodo . . . capite XXVII ejus libri . . . cui titulum fecit Compendium Legum Maritimarum," it was first printed in 1872 and was translated into English in 1928.[14] This edition substantially reproduces this translation, except that quotations from *The Free Sea* and from Welwod's reply have been taken from the texts printed in this edition.

---

13. A collotype of the original manuscript is available in Grotius, *Mare Liberum* (New York, 1952), a compendium of facsimiles assembled for an abortive edition of *Mare Liberum* by the Carnegie Endowment for International Peace.

14. Hugo Grotius, "Defensio capitis quinti Maris Liberi oppugnati a Guilielmo Welwodo . . . capite XXVII ejus libri . . . cui titulum fecit Compendium Legum Maritimarum" (ca. 1615), in Samuel Muller, *Mare Clausum: Bijdrage tot de Geschiedenis der Rivaliteit van Engeland en Nederland in de Zeventiende Eeuw* (Amsterdam: F. Muller, 1872), 331–61; Grotius, "Defense of Chapter V of the *Mare Liberum*," in "Some Less Known Works of Hugo Grotius," trans. Herbert F. Wright, *Bibliotheca Visseriana* 7 (1928): 154–205.

ACKNOWLEDGMENTS

I am very grateful to Knud Haakonssen for his invitation to contribute this volume to the series "Natural Law and Enlightenment Classics" and for his advice and encouragement at every stage of the editorial process. This edition would not have been possible without the generosity of the Masters of the Bench of the Inner Temple, by whose kind permission Richard Hakluyt's translation of *Mare Liberum* is reproduced. The staff of the Inner Temple Library, in particular Adrian Blunt, facilitated access to the manuscript and provided crucial help with its decipherment.

I am much indebted to Martine van Ittersum for making the initial transcription of the Inner Temple manuscript and for putting her extensive knowledge of Grotius's colonial activities at my disposal. I am likewise grateful to Åsa Söderman for scrupulously transcribing Welwod's reply to Grotius, to Kelly De Luca for her invaluable help in tracing elusive references, and to David Roochnik for kindly checking the Greek quotations. During two memorable seminars at the Folger Shakespeare Library in Washington, D.C., Peter Borschberg and Benedict Kingsbury greatly enlightened me about Grotius's intellectual development and his theoretical significance.

As always, Joyce Chaplin has supported an occasionally flagging editor.

THE FREE SEA

∞ HUGO GROTIUS ∞

The Free Sea

or

*A Disputation Concerning the Right Which the
Hollanders Ought to Have to the Indian
Merchandise for Trading*

THE CHAPTERS OF THE
DISPUTATION

3

To the Princes and Free States
of the Christian World

It is no less ancient than a pestilent error wherewith many men (but they chiefly who abound in power and riches) persuade themselves, or (as I think more truly) go about to persuade, that right and wrong are distinguished not according to their own nature but by a certain vain opinion and custom of men. These men therefore think that both laws and show of equity were invented for this purpose: that their dissensions and tumults might be restrained who are born in the condition of obeying; but unto such as are placed in the height of fortune they say that all right is to be measured by the will and the will by profits. And it is not so great a wonder that this absurd opinion, and altogether contrary to nature, hath procured unto itself some little authority, seeing to that common disease of mankind (whereby, as vice, so we follow the defense thereof)[1] the craft and subtlety of flatterers is added, whereunto all power is subject.

But on the contrary part, in all ages there have been some wise and religious men (not of servile condition) who would pluck this persuasion out of the minds of simple men and convince the others, being defenders thereof, of impudency. For they declared God to be the creator and governor of the world, especially the father of the nature of man which, therefore not as other living creatures, he severed into divers kinds and divers differences, but would have them of one kind and to be contained under one name; and gave moreover the same beginning and the like composition of members, countenances turned each to other and speech also, and other instruments of imparting, that all might understand there was a natural society and kindred between them. And to this house or city built by

---

1. *quo sicut vitia ita vitiorum patrocinia sectamur:* "by which we follow vices and the defenders of those vices."

him that great prince and householder had written certain laws of his, not in brass or tables, but in the minds and senses of everyone, where they shall offer themselves to be read of the unwilling and such as refuse. By these laws both high and low are bound. It is no more lawful for kings to transgress these than for the common people to impugn the decrees of senators, senators to resist the edicts of presidents, and viceroys the laws and statutes of their kings, for those very laws of people and all cities flowed from that fountain; thence they received their sanctimony and majesty.

But as in man himself there are some things which are common with all, and other some whereby everyone is to be distinguished from other, so of those things which nature had brought forth for the use of man she would that some of them should remain common and others through every one's labor and industry to become proper. But laws were set down for both, that all surely might use common things without the damage of all and, for the rest, every man contented with his portion should abstain from another's.

If no one can be ignorant of these things, unless he cease to be a man, if the nations saw this to whom the light of nature only shined (who otherwise were dull sighted in discerning truth), what beseemeth ye to think and do who are princes and Christian people?

If any think it hard that those things should be exacted of him which the profession of so holy a name requireth (the least whereof is to abstain from injuries) surely everyone may know what his duty is by that which he commandeth another. There is none of you who would not publicly exclaim that everyone should be moderator and arbitrator in his own matter, who would not command all citizens to use rivers and public places equally and indifferently, who would not with all his power defend the liberty of going hither and thither and trading.

If that little society which we call a commonwealth is thought not to stand without this (and indeed cannot stand without it), why shall not the self-same things be necessary to uphold the society and concord of all mankind? If any man violate these ye are justly displeased and make them also examples according to the quality and greatness of the offence, for no other reason but because the state of empire and government can never be quiet where these things may everywhere be done. If so be a king offer injury and violence unto a king, and people unto peoples, doth it not concern the perturbation of the peace and quiet of that city and the injury of the great keeper and commander? This only is the difference, that as subordinate magistrates judge the people, you the magistrates, so the king of all the world hath commanded you to take notice and punish all other men's faults. Yours only he hath excepted to himself who, though he hath reserved to himself the highest degree of punishment, slow, secret and inevitable, yet hath he assigned two judges from himself to be always present in men's affairs, whom the most happy offender cannot escape: to wit, every man's own conscience and fame, or other men's estimation of them. These seats of judgement stand always open to them to whom other tribunals are shut up; to these the weak and poor complain; in these they that master others in strength are vanquished themselves who are licentious out of measure, who esteem that at a base rate which was bought with man's blood, who defend injuries with injuries, whose manifest wickedness must needs be both condemned by the consenting judgment of the good and also not to be absolved in the opinion of their own mind.

To both these judgment places we bring a new case. Not truly of sinks or gutters or joining one rafter in another (as private men's cases are wont to be), nor yet of that kind which is usual among the people, of the right of a field bordering upon us or of the possession of a river or island, but almost of the whole sea, of the right of navigation and the liberty of traffic. These things are litigious between the Spaniards and us: whether the huge and vast sea be the addition of one kingdom (and that not the greatest); whether it be lawful for any people to forbid people that are willing neither to sell, buy nor change nor yet to come together; and whether any man could ever give that which was never his or find that which was another's before, or whether the manifest injury of long time give any right.

In this disputation we offer the counters[2] to those who among the Spaniards are the principal doctors of the divine and humane law; and, to conclude, we desire the proper laws of Spain. If that prevail not, and covetousness forbid them to desist whom some reason convinceth, we appeal,

---

2. *calculum porrigimus:* "we deliver the counter" (pass the buck).

oh ye princes, to your majesty; we appeal to your upright conscience and fidelity, oh ye nations, how many soever you be, wheresoever dispersed.

We move no doubtful or entangled question, not of doubtful principles in religion, which seem to have much obscurity, which being so long disputed with so stout courage, have almost left this for certain amongst wise men: that truth is never less found than when consent is compelled; not of the state of our commonwealth and liberty scarce gotten but defended by taking arms, whereof they can rightly determine who have exactly known the country laws of the Belgae, their ancient customs, and that it was not made a kingdom against the laws but an earldom by the laws. In which question, notwithstanding necessity was driven from equal judges of extreme servitude,[3] making a more curious search the authority of the decree of so many nations became public; the confession of the adversaries, even to the malicious and ill-willers, left no matter of doubt.

But that which we here propound hath nothing common with these; it needeth no man's curious search; it dependeth not on the exposition of the Bible (whereof many understand not many things), not on the decrees of one people whereof the rest may justly be ignorant.

That law by whose prescript form we are to judge is not hard to be found out, being the same with all and easy to be understood, which being bred with everyone is engrafted in the minds of all. But the right which we desire is such as the king himself ought not deny unto his subjects, nor a Christian to infidels, for it hath his original from nature, which is an indifferent and equal parent to all, bountiful towards all, whose royal authority extendeth itself over those who rule the nations and is most sacred amongst them who have profited most in piety.

Understand this cause, oh yea, princes, and consider it, oh yea, people. If we demand any unjust thing, ye know of what account your authority and theirs who amongst you are nearer unto us hath always been with us: advise us, and we will obey. But if we have offended anything in this matter, we beseech you not to be offended; the hatred of mankind we pray not

---

3. *aequis judicibus extrema servitutis depulsa necessitas:* "extreme necessity having compelled just judges into submission."

against. But if the matter fall out otherwise, we leave it to your religion and equity what you censure of it and what is to be done.

In times past, among the milder people it was accounted great impiety to assail them by war who would put their cause to arbitrement; on the contrary part, they who would refuse so equal a condition were repressed by the common aid not as enemies of one but of all. Therefore to that purpose we have seen truces made and judges appointed, kings themselves and puissant nations accounted nothing so glorious and honorable as to restrain others' insolency and to support others' infirmity and innocence.

Which custom, if it were in use at this day, that men thought no human thing strange unto them, surely we might have a more quiet world, for the presumption of many would wax cold and they who now neglect justice for profit's sake should learn to forget injustice with their own loss.

But as in this cause peradventure we hope for that in vain, so this we verily believe: that things being well weighed, you will all think the delays of peace are no more to be imputed unto us than the causes of war, and therefore as hitherto you have been well-willers and favorable friends unto us so you will much more befriend us hereafter, than the which nothing more desired can befall them who think it the first part of felicity to do well and the other to be well reported.

The Free Sea, or a Disputation Concerning the Right Which the Hollanders Ought to Have to the Indian Trade

CHAPTER I

By the law of nations navigation is free for any to whomsoever

Our purpose is shortly and clearly to demonstrate that it is lawful for the Hollanders, that is the subjects of the confederate states of the Low Countries, to sail to the Indians as they do and entertain traffic with them. We will lay this certain rule of the law of nations (which they call primary) as the foundation, the reason whereof is clear and immutable: that it is lawful for any nation to go to any other and to trade with it.

God himself speaketh this in nature, seeing he will not have all those things, whereof the life of man standeth in need, to be sufficiently ministered by nature in all places and also vouchsafeth some nations to excel others in arts. To what end are these things but that he would maintain human friendship by their mutual wants and plenty, lest everyone thinking themselves sufficient for themselves for this only thing should be made insociable? Now it cometh to pass that one nation should supply the want of another by the appointment of divine justice, that thereby (as Pliny saith) that which is brought forth anywhere might seem to be bred with all;[1] therefore we hear poets speaking,

---

1. Pliny the Younger, *Panegyricus,* XXIX. 7.

> *nec vero terrae ferre omnes omnia possunt,*[2]

also:

> *excudent alii,*[3]

and so forth.

They, therefore, that take away this, take away that most laudable society of mankind; they take away the mutual occasions of doing good and, to conclude, violate nature herself. For even that ocean wherewith God hath compassed the Earth is navigable on every side round about, and the settled or extraordinary blasts of wind, not always blowing from the same quarter, and sometimes from every quarter, do they not sufficiently signify that nature hath granted a passage from all nations unto all? This Seneca thinketh the greatest benefit of nature, that even by the wind she hath mingled nations scattered in regard of place and hath so divided all her goods into countries that mortal men must needs traffic among themselves.[4] This right therefore equally appertaineth to all nations, which the most famous lawyers enlarge so far that they deny any commonwealth or prince to be able wholly to forbid others to come unto their subjects and trade with them.[5] Hence descendeth that most sacred law of hospitality; hence complaints,

> *quod genus hoc hominum, quaeve hunc tam barbara morem*
> *permittit patria? hospitio prohibemur arenae,*[6]

and in another place,

> *litusque rogamus*
> *innocuum, et cunctis undamque auramque patentem.*[7]

---

2. "Nor yet can all soils bear all fruit": Virgil, *Georgics,* II, 109.

3. "Others shall beat [the breathing bronze]": Virgil, *Aeneid,* VI, 847.

4. Seneca, *Naturales quaestiones,* V. 18. 4.

5. *Institutes,* II. 1. 1; *Digest,* I. 8. 4; Gentili, *De jure belli,* I. 19; *Code,* IV. 63. 4.

6. "What race of men, and what land is so barbarous as to permit this custom? We are debarred the welcome of the beach": Virgil, *Aeneid,* I, 539–40.

7. "[We] now crave a harmless landing-place, and air and water free to all": Virgil, *Aeneid,* VII, 229–30.

We know also that wars began for this cause, as with the Magarensians against the Athenians,[8] and the Bononians against the Venetians,[9] and that these also were just causes of war to the Castilians against the Americans, and more probable than the rest. Victoria also thinketh it a just cause of war if they should be forbidden to go on pilgrimage and to live with them; if they were denied from the participation of those things which by the law of nations or customs are common; if, finally, they were not admitted to traffic.[10]

The like whereof is that which we read in the history of Moses, and Augustine thereupon: that the Israelites made just war against the Amorites because a harmless passage was denied which by the most just law of human society ought to have been open to them.[11] And for this cause Hercules made war with the King of the Orchomenians,[12] the Grecians under Agamemnon with the king of the Mysians, as if naturally (as Baldus saith) ways and passage should be free,[13] and the Romans in Tacitus are accused of the Germans because they barred the conference and resort of the nations and shut up rivers and earth and heaven itself after a certain manner.[14] Nor did any title against the Saracens in times past please the Christians better than that they were stopped by them from entering into the land of Jewry.[15]

It followeth upon this opinion that the Portugals, although they had been lords of those countries whither the Hollanders go, yet they should do wrong if they stopped the passage and trade of the Hollanders.

How much more unjust is it therefore for any that are willing to be secluded from intercourse and interchange with people who are also willing,

---

8. Diodorus Siculus, *Bibliotheca historica*, XII. 39; Plutarch, *Pericles*, XXIX.

9. Sigonio, *De regno Italiae*, XX.

10. Vitoria, *De Indis*, III. 1–2; Covarruvias, on *Sext*, rule *Peccatum*, § 9, n. 4: word *Quinta*.

11. Numbers 21: 22–25; Augustine, *Questions on Heptateuch*, IV, qu. 44, cit. *Decretum*, II. 23. 2. 3.

12. Apollodorus, *Library*, II. 7. 7 (referring to Amyntor, king of Ormenium).

13. Baldus, *Consilia*, III. 293.

14. Tacitus, *Histories*, IV. 64.

15. Alciati, *Consilia*, VII. 130; Covarruvias on *Sext*, rule *Peccatum*, Pt. II, § 10; Bartolus on *Code*, I. II. 1.

and that by their means in whose power neither these people are nor the thing itself whereby we make our way, seeing we detest not thieves and pirates more for any other cause than that they beset and molest the meetings of men among themselves?

CHAPTER 2

That the Portugals have no right of dominion over those Indians to whom the Hollanders sail by title of invention

But that the Portugals are not lords of those parts whither the Hollanders go—to wit, of Java, Tabrobana[1] and the greatest part of the Moluccas—we gather by a most certain argument, because no man is lord of that thing which neither he himself ever possessed nor any other in his name. These islands we speak of have, and always had, their kings, their commonwealth, their laws and their liberties. Trading is granted to the Portugals as to other nations; therefore, when they both pay tribute and obtain liberty of trade of the princes, they testify sufficiently that they are not lords but arrive there as foreigners, for they do not so much as dwell there but by entreaty. And although title be not sufficient for dominion, because possession also is required, seeing it is one thing to have a thing, another to have right to obtain it, yet I affirm that the Portugals have not so much as a title of dominion over those parts, which the opinion of the doctors (and those Spaniards) will not take from them.

First, if they will say those countries appertain unto them for a reward of the finding, they shall speak nor law nor truth, for to find is not to see a thing with the eyes but to lay hold of it with the hands, as in the epistle of Gordianus is declared.[2] Whence the grammarians use the words *inve-*

---

1. Classically identified with Ceylon (Sri Lanka) but Grotius uses it to mean the "island . . . which is now called Sumatra" (*De Jure Praedae,* 184).
2. *Code,* VIII. 41. 13.

nire and *occupare* for words of one signification, and all the Latin tongue saith, "we have found that which we have gotten," the contrary whereof is to lose.[3] Moreover, even natural reason itself and the express words of the laws and the interpretation of the most learned show that such a finding sufficeth to get title of common as is joined with possession:[4] to wit, movable things are laid hold on or immovable things are bounded and guarded,[5] which in this kind can no way be said, for the Portugals have no garrisons there. How can it be said by any means that the Portugals have found out India which was so famous many ages since, even from the time of Horace?[6]

> *impiger extremos currit mercator ad Indos*
> *per mare pauperiem fugiens.*[7]

How exactly have the Romans described many things unto us of Taprobane?[8] Now, as touching the other islands, not only the borderers, the Persians and Arabians, but the Europeans also (especially the Venetians), knew them before the Portugals.

Besides, the finding of them gives no right but in that which was no man's before their finding.[9] But the Indians, when the Portugals came unto them, although they were partly idolaters, partly Mahometans, and entangled in grievous sins, yet had they both publicly and privately authority over their own substance and possessions which without just cause could not be taken from them.[10] So with most sound reasons (following other authors of greatest account) the Spaniard Victoria concludeth, "Sec-

---

3. Nonius Marcellus, *De compendiosa doctrina,* IV, *s.v.* 'occupare'; Connan, *Commentarii juris civilis,* III. 3.

4. Doneau, *Commentarii juris civilis,* IV. 10; *Institutes,* II. 1. 13.

5. *Digest,* XLI. 2. 3, § 3.

6. The manuscript continues at this point, *Alia enim India, alia America ratio est:* "For there is one reason for India, another for America" (*De Jure Praedae,* fol. 98r).

7. "The ardent trader rushes to the furthest Indies, fleeing poverty across the sea": Horace, *Epistles,* I. 1. 45–46.

8. Pliny the Elder, *Natural History,* VI. 24. 81–91.

9. *Digest,* XLI. 1. 3.

10. Covarruvias on *Sext,* rule *Peccatum,* Pt. II, § 10, nn. 2, 4, 5.

ular or ecclesiastical Christians," saith he, "cannot deprive infidels of their equal power and sovereignty for that color only because they are infidels, unless some injury proceeded from them before."[11] "For faith," as Thomas saith well, "doth not take away natural or human law from whence dominion proceedeth; nay, it is a point of heresy to believe that infidels are not lords of their own goods, and to take from them their goods which they possess for this very cause is theft and robbery no less than if the same be done to Christians."[12]

Victoria therefore rightly saith that the Spaniards got no more authority over the Indians for this cause than the Indians had over the Spaniards if any of them had come formerly into Spain. Nor truly are the Indians out of their wits and unsensible but ingenious and sharp-witted, so that no pretence of subjecting them may be taken from hence, which notwithstanding by itself is sufficient manifest iniquity.[13] Plutarch long since calleth it πρόφασιν πλεονεξίας ἡμερῶσαι τὰ βαρβαρικά, to wit, a wicked desire of that which is another's, to pretend this color to himself that he may tame the barbarians.[14] And now also that color of bringing the gentiles against their will to a more civil kind of behavior, which the Grecians in times past and Alexander used, is thought wicked and impious of all divines, but specially the Spaniards.[15]

CHAPTER 3

That the Portugals have no right of dominion over the Indians by title of the Pope's gift

Secondly, if they will use the division of Pope Alexander the Sixth, above all that is specially to be considered whether the Pope would only decide

11. Vitoria, *De potestate civili*, I. 6.
12. Aquinas, *Summa Theologiae*, IIaIIae, q. 10, a. 12.
13. Vitoria, *De Indis*, I. 4–6.
14. Plutarch, *Pompey*, LXX. 3.
15. Vázquez, *Controversiae illustres*, Preface, 5–7.

the controversies of Portugals and Spaniards, which surely he might do as
a chosen arbitrator between them as the kings themselves had made certain covenants between them concerning that matter, and if it be so when
the thing was done between others, it appertaineth not to the rest of the
nations;[1] or whether he would give almost all the third part of the world
to two peoples, which though the Pope could and would have done, yet
shall it not presently follow that the Portugals are lords of those places,
seeing their donation maketh not the lords but the livery[2] which followeth, for even to this cause possession ought to be added.[3]

Moreover, if any man will search the law itself either divine or human
and not measure it by his private commodity, he shall easily find such a
kind of donation of that which is another's to be of no moment. I will not
here enter into disputation concerning the authority of the Pope, to wit,
the bishop of the Church of Rome, nor will I absolutely set down anything
but by hypothesis, to wit what the most learned men amongst them confess who attribute most to the authority of the Pope, chiefly the Spaniards
who, considering through their quickness of wit and understanding they
might easily see our lord Christ had rejected all earthly government,[4] he
had not truly dominion over the whole world as he was man, and if he had
yet could it not be proved by any argument that such right was translated
unto Peter or the Church of Rome by the right of vicar; seeing elsewhere
also it is certain Christ had many things unto the which the Pope succeeded not,[5] the interpreters affirmed (I will use their own words) that the
Pope is not a civil or temporal lord of the whole world;[6] yea, and that more
is, if he had any such authority in the world, yet should he not rightly exercise the same, seeing he ought to content himself with his spiritual juris-

---

1. Osório, *De rebus Emmanuelis*, fol. 323b.
2. *traditio:* delivery.
3. *Institutes*, II. 1. 40.
4. Luke, 12:14; John, 18:36; Vitoria, *De Indis*, II. 2.
5. Vitoria, *De Indis*, II. 2.
6. Vázquez, *Controversiae illustres*, I. 21. 1–3; Torquemada, *Summa de ecclesia*, II. 113;
Hugo of Pisa, *Summa on Decretum*, XCVI. 6; Bernard of Clairvaux, *De consideratione
ad Eugenium*, II. 6. 9–11; Vitoria, *De Indis*, II. 2; Covarruvias on *Sext*, rule *Peccatum*,
Pt. II, § 9, n. 7.

diction but could by no means grant it unto secular princes.[7] So then if he have any temporal authority he hath it (as they say) by way of order unto spiritual things, wherefore he hath no authority over infidels seeing they appertain not unto the Church.[8]

Whence it followeth, by the opinion of Cajetanus and Victoria and the better part as well divines as canonists, that it is not a sufficient title against the Indians either because the Pope gave those provinces as absolute lord or because they do not acknowledge the dominion of the Pope, so that the very Saracens were never spoiled under this color and pretence.[9]

CHAPTER 4

That the Portugals have no right of dominion over the Indians by title of war

These things therefore being taken away, seeing it is manifest (which even Victoria writeth) that the Spaniards' sailing to those remote countries brought no right with them of possessing those provinces, one only title of war remaineth which, though it had been just, yet could not profit them for dominion but by the right of prey, to wit, after the possession.[1] But it is so far from the matter that the Portugals possessed those things that they had no war at that time with many nations to whom the Hollanders went and so therefore no right could be gotten to them when also, if they had received any injuries from the Indians, they are supposed to have forgiven them by reason of the long peace and friendly traffic with them.

7. Matthew 17:25–27, 20:26; John 6:15.

8. Vitoria, *De Indis*, II. 2; Covarruvias on *Sext*, rule *Peccatum*, Pt. II, § 9, n. 7; I Corinthians 5:12–13.

9. Aquinas, *Summa Theologiae*, IIaIIae, q. 12, a 2; Ayala, *De jure*, I. 2. 29; Cajetan on Aquinas, *Summa Theologiae*, IIaIIae, q. 66, a. 8; Sylvester Prierias, *Summa Sylvestrina*, on *infidelitate et infidelibus*, VII; Innocent on *Decretum*, III. 34. 8; Vitoria, *De Indis*, II. 2.

1. Vitoria, *De Indis*, II. 2.

Although there were no cause truly that they should pretend war. For they who pursue the barbarians with war, as the Spaniards do the people of America, are wont to pretend two things: that they are hindered from trading with them, or because they will not acknowledge the doctrine of true religion.[2] As for trading, the Portugals obtained it of the Indians, so that in this behalf they have no reason to complain. The other pretence is no juster than that of the Grecians against the barbarians whereat Boethius aimed:

> *an distant, quia dissidentque mores,*
> *injustas acies, et fera bella movent,*
> *alternisque volunt perire telis?*
> *non est justa satis saevitiae ratio.*[3]

But this is the conclusion both of Thomas and the Council of Toledo, and Gregory and the divines and canonists and almost all the civilians:[4] although faith be declared to the barbarians (for concerning those who were subject before to Christian princes and also of apostates, the question is otherwise) probably and sufficiently and they will not respect it, yet notwithstanding it is not lawful for this reason to pursue them with wars and spoil them of their goods.[5]

It is needful to set down the very words of Cajetan to this purpose:

Certain infidels (saith he) neither in law nor in deed are subject to Christian princes as touching temporal jurisdiction, as they are found pagans who never were subject to the empire of Rome, inhabiting countries where the Christian name never came. For the lords thereof, although infidels, are lawful lords, whether they be governed by regal or politic government, neither are they deprived of the dominion of their lands or

---

2. Vázquez, *Controversiae illustres,* I. 24. 1–5; Vitoria, *De Indis,* II. 4.

3. "Is it because they differ and their customs disagree, that they unjustly wage such cruel wars and by each others' weapons are willing to die? Not right enough is cruelty's reasoning": Boethius, *De consolatione philosophiae,* IV. 4. 7–10.

4. Aquinas, *Summa Theologiae,* IIaIIae, q. 10, a. 8; *Decretum,* I. 45. 5, 3; Innocent on *Decretum,* I. 45. 5, 3; Bartolus on *Code,* I. 11. 1; Covarruvias on *Sext,* rule *Peccatum,* Pt. II, § 9–10; Ayala, *De jure,* I. 2. 28.

5. Matthew 10:23.

goods for their infidelity, seeing dominion is by a positive law and infidelity by the divine law which taketh not away the law positive, as is handled in the question before. And touching these, I know no law concerning temporal things. Against these no king, no emperor, nor the Church of Rome itself, can make war to possess their countries or subdue them temporally because there is no just cause of war, seeing Jesus Christ, the king of kings, to whom power is given in heaven and in earth, hath not sent soldiers of an armed warfare to take possession of the world but holy preachers as sheep among wolves. Whereupon I do not read in the Old Testament where possession was to be taken by arms that war was proclaimed against any country of the infidels because they were infidels but because they would not grant passage or because they had offended them, as the Midianites, or that they might recover their own granted unto them by the divine liberality. Wherefore we should grievously offend if we went about to spread the faith of Jesus Christ by this means, nor should we be lawful lords over them but should commit great robberies and were bound to make restitution as unjust conquerors and possessors. Good preachers should be sent unto them who by the word and their good example should convert them unto God, and not such as might oppress, spoil, offend and conquer them and make them twice more the children of hell after the manner of the Pharisees.[6]

And after this manner we hear it hath been often decreed by the senate in Spain and divines (but chiefly the Dominicans) that the Americans are to be converted to the faith by the preaching of the word only and not by war, and that the liberty also which had been taken from them for that cause should be restored, which is said to be approved of Paulus III the Pope and the emperor Charles the Fifth, king of Spain.[7]

We omit to speak that the Portugals now in most parts promote not religion nor so much as do there endeavor, seeing they are wholly bent to lucre, nay and that also to be true there which a Spaniard writ of the Spaniards of America, that no miracles, no signs and tokens, are to be heard of, no examples of a religious life which might vehemently per-

---

6. Cajetan on Aquinas, *Summa theologiae*, IIaIIae, q. 4, 66, a. 8.
7. Jean Matal, "Preface," fol. 15b, in Osório, *De rebus Emmanuelis.*

suade others to the same faith, but many scandals, many wicked deeds, many impieties.[8]

Wherefore, seeing both possession and title of possession fail, neither the substance nor jurisdiction of the Indians should be accounted in that nature as if they had been no man's before, neither seeing they were theirs could be rightly gotten by others. It follows that the peoples of India of whom we speak are not proper to the Portugals but free and in their own power, whereof the very Spanish doctors themselves make no question.

CHAPTER 5

That the sea or right of sailing on it is not proper to the Portugals by title of possession

If then the Portugals obtained no right over the people, countries, and jurisdictions, let us see whether they can make the sea and navigation or traffic to be in their power. Let us first consider of the sea which, seeing it is everywhere said to be no man's right, or common, or the public right of nations, what these words signify shall be most fitly declared if, following all poets from Hesiodus and philosophers and ancient civilians, we distinguish those things into times, which peradventure not a long time, yet notwithstanding by certain reason and their nature, are distinguished. Neither are we to be blamed if in the explanation of the law of nature we use their authority and words who (as it is manifest) were most powerful in the judgment of nature.

We are to know, therefore, in the first beginning of the life of man, dominion was another thing and communion differing from that which they are now.[1] For now dominion properly signifieth that which so appertaineth unto one that after the same manner it cannot be another's, but we

---

8. Vitoria, *De Indis,* II. 4.
1. Glossators and Castrensis on *Digest,* I. 1. 5; Glossators on *Decretum,* I. 1. 7.

call that common whose propriety is conferred among many with a certain fellowship and agreement excluding the rest. The defect of tongues hath enforced to use the same words in a thing which was not the same. And so these names of our custom are referred to that ancient law by a certain similitude and resemblance. That, therefore, which at that time was common was no other thing than that which is simply opposed unto proper. But dominion is a just or lawful power to use a common thing, which it seemed good to the Schoolmen to call *usum facti, non juris* because that use which is now called use in law or right is a certain propriety, or (that I may speak after their manner) is said privatively unto others.[2]

By the first law of nations, which sometimes also is called natural and which the poets elsewhere describe in the golden age, and in another place in the kingdom of Saturn or Justice, nothing was proper, which Cicero affirmed: "For by nature nothing is private."[3] And Horace:

> *nam proprie telluris herum natura nec illum,*
> *nec me, nec quemquam statuit.*[4]

For nature could not distinguish lords. In this signification, therefore, we affirm all things common at that time, signifying the same thing which the poets do when they say the first men sought the middle and justice held the middle of things by a chaste and inviolable covenant; which, that they might more plainly express, they deny that the fields were divided by bounds at that time or that there was any traffic:

> *promiscua rura per agros*
> *praestiterant cunctis communia cuncta videri.*[5]

This word *videri* is rightly added by reason of the translation of the word as we have said. But this communion was referred unto use:

---

2. Vázquez, *Controversiae illustres,* I. 17. 6–8; *Sext,* V. 12. 3; *Constitutions of Clement,* V. 11. 1.

3. Cicero, *De officiis,* I. 8. 21.

4. "Nature, in truth, makes neither him nor me nor anyone else lord of the soil as his own": Horace, *Satires,* II. 2. 129–30.

5. "The farms scattered throughout the fields showed that all things seemed common to everyone": Avienus, *On Aratus' Phaenomena,* 302–3.

pervium cunctis iter,
communis usus omnium rerum fuit.[6]

By reason whereof there was a certain kind of dominion, but universal and indefinite. For God gave all things not to this man or that but to mankind and after that manner many may be wholly lords of the same thing; but if we take dominion in that signification which it hath at this day it is against all reason, for this includeth a propriety which then no man had. But that is most aptly spoken:

omnia rerum
usurpantis erant.[7]

But it seemeth we are come to that distinction of dominions which is now not violent but by little and little, nature showing the beginning thereof. For seeing there are many things the use whereof consisteth in abuse, or for that being converted into the substance of the user they admit no use after, or because by use they are made worse for use, in things of the former kind, as meat and drink, a certain propriety appeared not severed from use.[8] For this is to be proper, so to appertain to any that it cannot also be another's, which afterwards by a certain reason was derived to things of the latter kind, to wit, garments and chattels or movables; which being so, all immovable things—to wit, fields—could not remain undivided, although the use of them consist not simply in abuse, yet the use thereof was procured by reason of some abuse, as ploughed fields and orchards of fruit trees for food, pastures also for raiment, but they could not in common suffice for the use of all people. Property being found out, there was a law set down which should imitate nature. For, as in the beginning that use was had by corporal application whence, we said before, property had his original, so by the like application it seemed good they should be made the proper goods of everyone. This is that which is called

---

6. "Open to all the way, in common was the use of every thing": Seneca, *Octavia*, 402–3.

7. "All things belonged to anyone who could take them": Avienus, *On Aratus' Phaenomena*, 301–2.

8. *Digest*, VII. 5; Pope John XXII, *Extravagantes tum Viginti Joannis Papae XXII tum Communes*, XIV. 3, 5; Aquinas, *Summa Theologiae*, IIaIIae, q. 78, a. 1.

occupation by a word most aptly applied unto those things which before were indifferent. Whereunto the tragedian Seneca alludeth,

> *in medio est scelus*
> *positum occupanti,*[9]

and the philosopher, "All things pertaining to the Horsemen belonged to the gentlemen of Rome, yet amongst them is my proper place which I possessed."[10] Hereupon Quintilian saith it is natural to all that there should be a reward of industry and Tully that things by ancient occupation became theirs who in times past succeeded into the goods of the dead.[11] But this occupation in those things which resist possession, as wild beasts, ought to be perpetual; in other things it sufficeth that a corporal possession begun be retained in the mind. Occupation or possession in movables is apprehension; in immovables, instruction and limitation. Whereupon when Hermogenianus saith they were distinct dominions he added that the fields were bounded and houses built.[12] This state of things is declared of poets:

> *tum laqueis captare feras, et fallere visco*
> *inventum;*[13]
>
> *tum primum subiere domos;*[14]
>
> *communemque prius, ceu lumina solis et aurae*
> *cautus humum longo signavit limite messor.*[15]

After these things, intercourse of merchandise began to come in use, for which cause,

> *fluctibus ignotis insultavere carinae.*[16]

---

9. "Between us lies the crime for him who first shall do it": Seneca, *Thyestes,* 203–4.

10. Seneca, *De beneficiis,* VII. 12. 3.

11. Quintilian, *Declamations,* XIII. 8; Cicero, *De officiis,* I. 7. 21.

12. *Digest,* I. 1. 5.

13. "Then men found how to snare game in toils and to cheat with birdlime": Virgil, *Georgics,* I, 139–40.

14. "In that age men first sought the shelter of houses": Ovid, *Metamorphoses,* I, 121.

15. "And the ground, which had hitherto been a common possession like the sunlight and the air, the careful surveyor now marked out with a long-drawn boundary line": Ovid, *Metamorphoses,* I, 135–36.

16. "Keels . . . leaped insolently over unknown waves": Ovid, *Metamorphoses,* I, 134.

The same time commonwealths began to be instituted and established. And so of those which were divided or separated from the first common two kinds are made, for some things are public, to wit, proper to the people (which is the double signification of this word), some things mere private, to wit, proper to every particular man. But occupation is made public after the same manner that it is made private. Seneca saith, "we call those the bounds of the Athenians or Campanians which afterward the borderers divide among themselves by private bounds."[17] For every nation,

> *partita fines regna constituit, novas*
> *extruxit urbes.*[18]

After this manner Cicero saith, "the territory of the Arpinates is called Arpinatum, of the Tusculans, Tusculanum; the like description," saith he, "is of private possessions, whereupon because every man's own consisteth of those things which by nature were common, let every man hold that which fell to his share."[19] But contrariwise Thucydides calleth that land which fell to no people in division ἀοριστον, to wit, indefinite.[20]

Of these things which hitherto have been spoken two things may be gathered. The first is that those things which cannot be occupied or were never occupied can be proper to none because all propriety hath his beginning from occupation.[21] The other is that all those things which are so ordained by nature that anyone using them they may nevertheless suffice others whomsoever for the common use are at this day (and perpetually ought to be) of the same condition whereof they were when nature first discovered them. Cicero meaneth this when he saith, "This society among all showeth itself far to all men among themselves, in the which a community of all those things which nature brought forth for the common use is to be preserved."[22] But all things are of this kind, wherein without the

17. Seneca, *De beneficiis,* VII. 4. 3.
18. " . . . marking out boundaries, established kingdoms, built new cities": Seneca, *Octavia,* 420–21.
19. Cicero, *De officiis,* I. 7. 21.
20. Thucydides, *Histories,* I. 139. 2.
21. Douaren on *Digest,* I. 8.
22. Cicero, *De officiis,* I. 16. 51.

damage of one another may be pleasured. Hence, saith Cicero, is that "not to forbid running water."[23] For running water as it is such, not as it is a river, is acknowledged of the civilians to be in the number of those things which are common to all; and of the poet,

> *quid prohibetis aquas? usus communis aquarum est.*
> *nec solem proprium natura, nec aera fecit,*
> *nec tenues undas: in publica munera veni.*[24]

He affirmeth these things not to be proper by nature—as Ulpian saith, they lie open to all by nature[25]—both because they were first discovered by nature and never came as yet into the dominion of any (as Neratius speaketh),[26] and also because (as Cicero saith) they seem to be brought forth of nature for the common use.[27] But he calleth those things public by a translated signification, not which appertain to any one country and people but to the whole society of mankind, which in the laws are called *publica juris gentium:* that is, common to all and proper to none.[28] Of this kind the air is for a double reason, both because it cannot be possessed and also because it oweth a common use to men. And for the same cause the element of the sea is common to all, to wit, so infinite that it cannot be possessed and applied to all uses, whether we respect navigation or fishing.[29] Whose ever the sea is, theirs also are those things which the sea, taking away from others' uses, hath made for own, as the sands of the sea, part whereof joining to the land is called the shore. Cicero therefore saith well, "what is so common as the sea to them that float thereon and the

---

23. Cicero, *De officiis,* I. 16. 52.

24. "Why do you deny me water? The enjoyment of water is a common right. Nature has not made the sun private to any, nor the air, nor soft water: the common right I seek": Ovid, *Metamorphoses,* VI, 349–51.

25. *Digest,* VIII. 4. 13.

26. *Digest,* XLI. 1. 14.

27. Cicero, *De officiis,* I. 16. 51.

28. Connan, *Commentaria juris civilis libri X,* III. 2; Doneau, *Commentarii de jure civili,* IV. 2; *Digest,* XLI. 3. 45.

29. *Digest,* I. 8. 2.

shore for them that are cast out."[30] Virgil also saith that the air, the water and the shore lie open unto all.[31]

These things therefore are those which the Romans call common unto all by the laws of nature, or which are said to be the same *publica juris gentium,* as also they call the use of them sometimes common and sometimes public.[32] But although even those things are rightly said to be no man's as touching the property, yet they differ much from those things which are no man's and are not attributed to common use, as wild beasts, fishes and birds. For if any man possess these they may become his proper right, but those things by the consent of all mankind are perpetually exempted from propriety for use which, seeing it belongeth to all, it can no more be taken away by one from all than you may take away that from me which is mine. This is that which Cicero saith, that it is among the first or chief duties of justice to use common things for common things.[33] The Schoolmen would say that some things are common affirmatively and some privatively. This distinction is not only very common among the civilians but also it expresseth the confession of the common people, whereupon the master of the feast in Athenaeus saith the sea was common but the fishes theirs that could take them. And in Plautina, to one that said unto him, keeping his cable,[34] "The sea was common for all," the fisherman consented, but when he added, "It was found in the sea; it is common," it came well to hand: "That which my net and hooks have gotten is principally mine."[35]

The sea therefore cannot be altogether proper unto any because nature doth not permit but commandeth it should be common, no nor so much as the shore,[36] but that this interpretation is to be added: that if any of

---

30. Cicero, *Pro Roscio,* XXVI. 72.

31. Virgil, *Aeneid,* VII. 230.

32. *Institutes,* II. 1. 1, 5; *Digest,* I. 8. 1, 2, 10; *Digest,* XLI. 1. 14; *Digest,* XLVII. 10. 13, § 7; *Digest,* XLIII. 8. 3, 4.

33. Cicero, *De officiis,* I. 7. 20.

34. *Et in Plautina Rudente servato dicenti:* "And in Plautus's *The Rope,* when the servant said. . . ."

35. Plautus, *The Rope,* IV. 3. 975, 977, 985.

36. Doneau, *Commentarii de jure civili,* IV. 2.

those things by nature may be occupied, that may so far forth become the occupant's as by such occupation the common use be not hindered. Which is worthily received and approved, for seeing it is so, both exceptions cease whereby we said it came to pass that all things should not be transferred to proper right.

Because therefore building is a kind of occupation, it is lawful to build upon the shore if it may be without the hurt of the rest, as Pomponius speaketh, which we will expound out of Scaevola, unless the public, that is to say, the common use should be hindered.[37] And he which hath built shall become lord of the soil because that ground was proper to none nor necessary for the common use; it is therefore the occupant's, but no longer than the occupation continueth, because the sea seemeth to resist possession, by the example of a wild beast which, if it betake itself to the natural liberty, is no longer his who was the taker; so also the shore, which afterward giveth place unto the sea again.[38]

But whatsoever may become private by occupation we have declared that the same may also become public, that is to say, proper to the people. So Celsus thinketh that the shore enclosed within the bounds of the empire of Rome appertaineth to the people of Rome;[39] which, if it be so, it is no marvel that the same people could grant a means (by their prince or praetor) to their subjects how to possess the shore.[40] But even this occupation, no less than private, is so to be restrained that it stretch no further than that the public use may be preserved. No man therefore may be forbidden by the people of Rome to come unto the sea-shore and to dry their nets and do other things which once all men would have perpetually to be lawful for them.[41]

But the nature of the sea differeth in this from the shore in that the sea, unless it be in some small part thereof, cannot easily be built upon nor can be included, and though it could, yet this notwithstanding should scarce

37. *Institutes*, II. 1, § 5; *Digest*, I. 8. 5, § 1; *Digest*, XXXIX. 2. 24; *Digest*, XLI. 1. 50; *Digest*, XLIII. 8. 4.
38. *Digest*, I. 8. 10; *Digest*, XLI. 1. 14.
39. *Digest*, XLIII. 8. 3; Doneau, *Commentarii de jure civili*, IV. 2, 9.
40. *Digest*, XLI. 1. 50; *Digest*, XLIII. 8. 2, §§ 10, 16.
41. *Digest*, I. 8. 5; *Digest*, XLIII. 8. 3.

happen without the impediment of the common use, yet if any little part may so be occupied it is granted to the occupant. It is therefore a hyperbole:

> contracta pisces aequora sentiunt
> iactis in altum molibus.[42]

For Celsus saith that planks or piles laid in the sea are his who laid them, but that is not to be granted if the use of the sea by that means shall become worse.[43] And Ulpian saith that he that dams up the sea is so to be allowed and defended if no man be hurt thereby.[44] For if this thing shall hurt any man surely he must be forbidden, that nothing be done in a public place.[45] As Labeo also saith, if any such thing be built in the sea he will have him forbidden, "that nothing be done in the sea whereby the haven, road or way for ships may be made the worse."[46]

And the same regard that is to be had of navigation is to be had likewise of fishing, that it may remain common unto all. Yet shall not he offend that encloseth a place of fishing for himself with stakes or piles in a creek of the sea and so maketh it private, as Lucullus who cut down a hill at Naples to let in the sea to his farm?[47] And of this kind I think the fishponds upon the sea-coast were whereof Varro and Columella make mention.[48] Neither did Martial mean otherwise when he speaketh of Formianus of Apollinaris:

> si quando Nereus sentit Aeoli regnum,
> ridet procellas tuta de suo mensa.[49]

---

42. "The fishes note the narrowing of the waters by piers of rock laid in their depths": Horace, *Odes*, III. 1. 33–34.

43. *Digest*, XLIII. 8. 3.

44. *Digest*, XLIII. 8. 2, § 8.

45. *interdictum utique, "Ne quid in loco publico" competiturum:* "the interdict, 'Ne quid in loco publico fiat' is to be enforced."

46. *Digest*, XLIII. 12. 1, § 17.

47. Varro, *De re rustica*, III. 17. 9.

48. Ibid., III. 2. 17; III. 3. 10.

49. "Should Nereus feel the power of Aeolus, the table, secure in its own store, laughs at storms": Martial, *Epigrams*, X. 30. 19–20.

And Ambrose: "Thou bringest the sea within thy manors lest monsters[50] should be wanting."[51] Hence it may appear of what mind Paul[us] was: "if the proper right of the sea appertain to any, as ye possess them,[52] he must be forbidden."[53] That this interdiction was ordained for private causes not for public, wherein also those things are comprehended which by the common law of nature we may do, but here the right of enjoying is handled which happeneth upon a private cause, not public or common. For Marcian testifieth whatsoever is possessed or may be possessed, that now appertaineth not to the law of nations as the sea doth:[54] as, for example, if any had forbid Lucullus or Apollinaris to fish in that which was private unto them in regard they enclosed a creek of the sea, Paulus thought they were to be forbidden, not only an action of trespass to be brought against them by reason of the private possession.

Nay, in a creek of the sea, as in a creek of a river, if I have possessed such a place and have fished there, specially if I have testified my purpose privately of possessing it by the continuance of many years, by that right I may forbid another to use the same (as we gather out of Marcian) no otherwise than in a lake in my jurisdiction, which is true so long as occupation continueth, as we said before of the shore.[55] The same shall not be without the creek lest the common use be hindered.[56]

It is a very usual thing therefore that men forbid any to fish before my house or the prince's palace, but by no right, so that Ulpian contemning that usurpation saith if any be forbid he may have an action of trespass.[57] The emperor Leo (whose laws we use not) changed this against the reason of the law and would have πρόθυρα, that is to say, the front of the sea, to be proper unto them who inhabited that coast, and that they have right of fishing there;[58] which yet he would have proceed so far, that the place

---

50. *belluae:* "wild animals."
51. Ambrose, *De Nabuthe*, III. 12.
52. *uti possidetis.*
53. *Digest,* XLVII. 10. 14.
54. *Digest,* I. 8. 4.
55. *Digest,* XLIV. 3. 7.
56. *Digest,* XLI. 3. 45.
57. *Digest,* XLVII. 10. 13, § 7.
58. Leo, *Novellae,* LVI.

should be possessed with certain stopping enclosures or sluices, which the Greeks call ἐποχας, thinking doubtless it should not come to pass that any should envy another a little portion of the sea who should be admitted himself to fish in the whole sea.[59] Surely, howsoever any take away a great part of the sea from public utility, although he be able to do it, it is intolerable wickedness against which the holy man Ambrose inveigheth: "They challenge unto themselves the length of the sea by the law of a bondslave, and mention the right of fishes as of slaves subject to them in a servile condition. This gulf of the sea," saith he, "is mine; that, another's. Thus mighty men divide the elements unto themselves."[60]

The sea therefore is in the number of those things which are not in merchandise and trading, that is to say, which cannot be made proper.[61] Whence it followeth, if we speak properly, no part of the sea can be accompted in the territory of any people. Which thing Placenti[n]us seemeth to have meant when he said, "That the sea was so common, that it may be in the dominion of none but God alone," and Johannes Faber, "When the sea shall depart, left in his ancient right and being, wherein all things were common," otherwise those things which are common to all shall differ nothing from those things which are properly called public, as the sea from a river.[62] The people of a country might possess a river as included within their bounds, but so could they not the sea.

But territories are of the possession of a people as private dominions are of the possessions of particular men. Celsus saw this, who clearly enough distinguisheth between the shores which the people of Rome might occupy, yet so that the common use should not be hurt and the sea which retained her ancient nature.[63] Neither doth any law show the contrary. But those laws which are cited out of authors of contrary opinion either speak concerning islands (which is clear might be possessed) or else concerning a haven, which is not common but properly public.[64]

---

59. Leo, *Novellae,* LVII, CII, CIII, CIV; Cujas, *Observationes,* XIV. 1.
60. Ambrose, *Hexaemeron,* V. 10. 27.
61. Doneau, *Commentarii de jure civili,* IV, 6.
62. Faber on *Institutes,* II. 1. 5; Doctors on *Digest,* XIV. 2. 9.
63. *Digest,* XLIII. 8. 3.
64. *Digest,* V. 1. 9; *Digest,* XXXIX. 4. 15.

But they who say that some sea appertaineth to the empire of Rome interpret their saying so that they affirm that right over the sea proceedeth not beyond protection and jurisdiction,[65] which right they distinguish from propriety; nor peradventure do they sufficiently observe that, in that the people of Rome might appoint a convoy for the aid and succor of such as passed the seas and punish such pirates as were taken on the sea, it happened not by any proper right but of the common right which also other free nations have in the sea. In the mean space we yet confess this that some nations might agree among themselves that such as were taken in this or that part should be judged by this or that commonwealth, and so for the benefit of distinguishing jurisdictions the bounds in the sea to be described, which truly bindeth the making that law to themselves which could not bind other people in like manner. Neither doth it make the place proper to any but conferreth the right upon the persons of the contractors.[66]

Which distinction, as it is agreeable to nature, so it was approved by a certain answer of Ulpian who, being demanded whether the lord of two manors upon the sea could impose servitude upon one of them which he would sell, that it should not thereby be lawful to fish in a certain place of the sea, answered the thing itself, that the sea could not have any servitude imposed on it because by nature it should be open to all, but seeing the true meaning of a contract required the law of sale to be kept, the persons of the possessors and such as succeeded in their right were bound by this law.[67] It is true that the lawyer spoke of private manors and a private law but in a territory and law of the people here is the same reason, because the people in respect of all mankind have the place of private men.

In like manner, the rents which are set down for fishing upon the seacoast are reckoned in the number of royalties, and bind not the thing, that is, the sea or fishing, but the persons.[68] Wherefore subjects over whom the commonwealth or prince have power to make a law by consent may peradventure be compelled to these burdens and impositions, but the right of

65. Glossators on *Digest,* I. 8. 2; Baldus and Glossators on *Institutes,* II. 1. 1, 5.
66. Baldus on *Feuds,* p. 19; *Code,* XI. 12; Angelus on *Digest,* XLVII. 10. 14.
67. *Digest,* VIII. 4. 13.
68. *Feuds,* II. 56.

fishing everywhere ought to be free to foreigners, that servitude be not imposed on the sea, which cannot serve.

For the reason of the sea and of a river is not the same, which seeing it is public, that is to say, the people's, the right also of fishing in it may be granted or letten by the people or prince,[69] so that they of ancient time gave a prohibition of enjoying a public place to him who hired it, adding a condition "if he who had the right of letting let it to any to enjoy," which condition cannot be in the sea.[70] But they that reckon fishing in the number of royalties did not sufficiently consider that place which they interpreted, whereof Isernia and Alvarotus were not ignorant.[71]

It hath been declared that neither the people nor any private man can have any property in the sea (for we excepted a creek), seeing neither the consideration of public use nor nature permitted occupation. And indeed this disputation was appointed for this purpose that it might appear the Portugals have not made the sea whereby we sail to the Indies to be in their jurisdiction. For both reasons which hinder propriety are infinitely more effectual in this case than in all the rest. That which in other things seemeth hard cannot be so at all in this; that which we judge unjust in others in this is most barbarous and inhuman.

We treat not here of an inland sea which here and there spreading itself upon the earth and somewhere also exceeds not the breadth of a river, whereof yet it is manifest the Roman lawyers spake when they uttered or published those noble sentences against private avarice. The question is concerning the whole ocean, which antiquity calleth unmeasurable and infinite, the parent of things bordering upon heaven, with whose perpetual moisture the ancients supposed not only fountains and rivers and seas, but also the clouds and the very stars themselves, in some sort to be maintained, which finally compassing the earth (this seat of mankind) by the reciprocal courses of tides can neither be kept back nor included and more truly possesseth than is possessed.

And in this ocean the controversy is not of a bay or narrow strait or

69. Balbus, *De praescriptionibus,* V. 4, q. 6, n. 4.
70. *Digest,* XLVII. 10. 13, § 7; *Digest,* XLIII. 9. 1.
71. On *Feuds,* rubric: *Quae sint regalia,* n. 72.

concerning all that may be seen from the shore. The Portugals challenge to themselves whatsoever lies between two worlds divided by so great distance that in many ages they could not from place to place convey the report of them. But if the portion of the Castilians (who are in the same case) be added, little less than the whole ocean is enthralled to two nations, so many other nations being brought to the narrow straits of the north, and nature is much deceived who, seeing she hath scattered this element over all, thought also it should suffice all. If any in so great a sea should take empire and jurisdiction wholly to himself from the common use, yet nevertheless he should be accompted an ambitious seeker of excessive dominion; if any should forbid others to fish, he could not escape the brand of the brainsick covetousness. But he that doth also hinder navigation whereby he loseth nothing, what shall we conclude of him?

If any should forbid another to take fire from his fire, which is wholly his, and light from his light, by the law of human society I would accuse and sue him to condemnation, because the force of this nature is such

ut nihilominus ipsi luceat, cum illi accenderit.[72]

What else, for when he may without his own damage let him impart unto another in such things as are profitable to the receiver and not offensive to the giver?[73]

These be the duties which the philosophers will have performed not only to strangers but also to the unthankful.[74] That which is envy in private things in a common thing cannot but be cruelty. For this is most wicked for thee so to intercept that which by the appointment of nature and by the consent of nations is no less mine than thine, that thou wilt not grant me so much as the use, which granted, that may be thine no less than it was before.

But then if they also who[75] violently take other men's goods and intercept common things defend themselves with a certain kind of possession.

---

72. "That no less will his [light] shine when he his [friend's] has lit": Ennius, cit. Cicero, *De officiis,* I. 16. 51.

73. Cicero, *De officiis,* I. 16. 51–52.

74. Seneca, *De beneficiis,* IV. 28.

75. *Tum vero etiam qui:* "But even they who. . . ."

For because (as we said) the first possession maketh things proper, therefore a detaining, although it be unjust, carrieth a certain kind of show of dominion. But whither have the Portugals compassed that sea with garrisons placed there, as we use to do the land, that so it should be in their power to exclude whom they would? Or whither is it so far off that they also, when they divide the world against other nations they defend themselves, not by any limits either by nature or set by hand but by a certain imaginary line? Which if it be allowed, and such a dimension be sufficient for possession, the geometricians should long since have taken away the earth from us and the astronomers heaven.

Where is therefore this adjoining of body to body, without which no dominion began? Surely that which our doctors have delivered appeareth not more truly spoken in anything: that seeing the sea is incomprehensible, no less than the air, it can be added to the goods of no nation.[76]

But if they call this possession, that they sailed before others and after a sort opened the way, what can be more ridiculous? For seeing there is no part of the sea into the which someone hath not entered first, it will follow that all navigation was possessed of some. So we are every way excluded. And they also who were carried about the whole world shall be said to have gotten the whole ocean to themselves. But no man is ignorant that a ship passing the seas leaveth no more right than the way thereof. But that they also assume unto themselves that no man sailed that ocean before them it is not true, for a great part of that sea whereof we speak, round about Mauritania, was long since sailed and that part of the sea beyond, bending toward the east, in the victories of Alexander the Great was compassed, even to the gulf of Arabia.[77]

There are also many arguments to prove that this voyage by sea was well known in times past to those people or islanders of Gades. Caius Caesar, the son of Augustus, having to do in the gulf of Arabia, the marks or tokens of ships remaining of the Spanish wrecks were known unto him of old, which also Caelius Antipater reported he saw, who sailed from Spain to Aethiopia for trade of merchandise, and to the Arabians also, if it be

---

76. Faber on *Institutes,* II. 1. 5.
77. Pliny, *Natural History,* II. 67, VI. 31; Pomponius Mela, *De situ orbis,* III. 17.

true which Cornelius Nepos witnesseth, that a certain man called Eudoxus
in his times, when he fled from Lathyrus, king of Alexandria, coming forth
of the Arabian Gulf, was brought to the islands Gades. It is most evident
also that the Carthaginians, who were well skilled in matters of the sea,
could not be ignorant of that ocean, seeing Hanno, when Carthage most
flourished, being carried about from Gades to the uttermost bounds of
Arabia, sailing by the promontory now called the Cape de Bona Esperanza
(whose ancient name seemeth to have been Hesperion Ceras), hath set
down all that voyage in writing with the situation of the shore and islands,
and witnesseth at last that not the sea but provisions failed him.

That also in the flourishing estate of Rome they were wont to sail from
the Arabian gulf to India and the islands of the Indian Ocean, even to
golden Chersonesus (which most men suppose to be Japan), the voyage
described of Pliny, the embassages from the Indies to Augustus, to Claudius also from the island Taprobane, besides the worthy acts of Trajan and
Ptolemy's tables, sufficiently declare.[78] Strabo witnesseth that even in his
time a fleet of Alexandrian merchants out of the Arabian Gulf sailed to the
furthest parts of Aethiopia, and so of India, when in times past few ships
durst attempt it.[79] Thereby the people of Rome had great revenues. Pliny
addeth that they sailed having shipped bands of archers for fear of pirates,
and that India alone took away yearly from the empire of Rome 500 ses-
tertia (if you add Arabia and Seres they took 1,000), and that the merchandise were sold for a hundredfold more.[80]

These ancient testimonies sufficiently argue that the Portugals were not
the first. That ocean in every particular part thereof, both then when the
Portugals first entered it and also before, was never unknown, for the
Moors, Aethiopians, Arabians, Persians, and Indians could no way be ignorant of that part of the sea whereof they were borderers. They therefore
speak untruly who boast that they first found out that sea.

What therefore shall any man say? Seemeth it a final matter that the
Portugals have renewed navigation first, intermitted peradventure so

78. Pliny, *Natural History*, VI. 24.
79. Strabo, *Geography*, II. 5. 12; XVII.
80. Pliny, *Natural History*, VI. 23; XII. 18 [Grotius's references].

many ages and (which cannot be denied) have discovered it unknown to
the nations of Europe through their great labor, cost and danger? Nay
truly, if this hath been all the care and endeavor, to show that to all which
they only have found, who is so mad that would not profess himself much
indebted unto them? For they should deserve the same thanks, praise and
immortal glory wherewith all discoverers of great matters have been contented, how many soever have endeavored not to benefit themselves but
mankind. But if the Portugals had their own gain before their eyes, gain
(which always is the greatest thing in perverting negotiations)[81] ought to
suffice them. For we know the first voyages sometimes have yielded forty-
fold increase or more, whereby it came to pass that a people who were long
time poor came suddenly to unexpected riches, in so great excess of riot[82]
as scarce befell the happiest nations in the highest degree of fortune's long
progress.

But if they went before in this, that no man should follow, they deserve
no thanks, seeing they respected their own gain, but they cannot call it
their gain when they take away that which is another's. Neither is that certain unless the Portugals had gone thither that no man would have gone,
for the times were at hand wherein, as almost all arts, so the situation of
seas and countries were daily more clearly known unto us. The ancient
examples which we now reported would have provoked us, and if all had
not been discovered at one clap yet by little and little the shores had been
descried by sailing, one shore always discovering another. Finally that had
come to pass which the Portugals hath taught us might be done, seeing
there were many nations no less inflamed with the desire of merchandise
and foreign commodities. The Venetians, who had learned many things
of India, would have been as ready to seek as the rest. The undaunted diligence of the Bretons of France and the stout courage of the English
should not have been wanting to this enterprise. And the Hollanders
themselves have attempted much more desperate matters.

No reason therefore of equity nor surely any probable opinion maketh
for the Portugals. For all they who will by possibility have the sea subject

81. *praevertendis negotiantibus:* "for those first in a new field of enterprise."
82. *tanto luxus apparatu:* "in such appearance of luxury."

to the command of any attribute it to him who have the next havens and bordering shores in his jurisdiction.[83] But the Portugals in that huge coast of shores have nothing except a few garrisons which they may call theirs.

Moreover, also he that should have authority over the sea could diminish nothing of the common use, as the people of Rome could hinder none from using all things in the shore of the empire of Rome which were permitted by the law of nations.[84] And if it could forbid any of those things, to wit, fishing, whereby it may be said after a sort that fishes should be taken, yet they could not forbid navigation, whereby the sea loseth nothing.

For proof whereof that which we have delivered by the opinion of doctors is a most certain argument: that on the land, which is given both to nations and every particular man in property, a quiet and harmless passage can justly be denied to no men of any nation, no more than drink out of a river. The reason appeareth because, seeing the uses of one thing were naturally divers, the nations only seem to have divided it among themselves, which cannot conveniently without property be had and contrarily he received it by whom the condition of the lord should not be made the worse.

All men therefore see that he who would forbid another to sail can defend himself by no law, seeing Ulpian saith he is guilty of wrong.[85] Others also thought that he that is forbid may have a prohibition.[86]

And so the intention of the Hollanders is grounded upon the common law, seeing all men confess that all men are permitted to sail in the sea though leave be obtained of no prince, which is plainly expressed in the Spanish laws.[87]

---

83. Glossators on *Sext,* I. 6. 3. 2; Glossators on *Decretum,* II. 9. 3.

84. *Digest,* I. 8. 4; Gentili, *De jure belli,* I. 19.

85. *Digest,* XLIII. 8. 2, § 9.

86. *interdictum utile prohibito competere:* "that the injunction *utile prohibito* might be brought against him"; Glossators on *Digest,* XLIII. 14. 1.

87. Baldus on *Digest,* I. 8. 3; Rodericus Suárez, *De usu maris,* I. 3; *Las Siete Partidas,* Pt. III, tit. 28, law 3.

CHAPTER 6

The sea or right of navigation is not proper to the Portugals by title of the Pope's gift

The donation of Pope Alexander, which may be alleged in the second place by the Portugals challenging the sea or right of sailing only to themselves, seeing the title of invention faileth, is sufficiently convinced of vanity by that which hath been spoken before. For donation hath no force in things which are without the compass of merchandise, wherefore, seeing the sea or the right of sailing in it can be proper to no man, it follows that it could neither be given by the Pope nor received of the Portugals. Further, seeing it is before declared by the opinion of all men of sound judgment that the Pope is not a temporal lord of the whole world, it is sufficiently understood that he is not lord of the sea. Although that be granted, yet the right annexed to the papacy should in no part be transferred to any king or people, as the emperor could not convert or alien at his pleasure the provinces of the empire to his own uses.[1]

That no man, at the least that hath any shame, will deny, seeing no man will grant the Pope right of disposing in temporal things unless peradventure so much as his necessity of spiritual things requireth, but these things whereof we now treat—to wit, the sea and the right of sailing—respect gain and mere profit, not the affairs of piety; it follows that his power in this was nothing. What, cannot princes indeed, that is temporal lords, by any means hinder any from navigation, seeing if they have any right in the sea it is only the right of protection and jurisdiction? That also is well known among all that the Pope hath no authority to do these things which are contrary to the law of nature.[2] But it is contrary to the law of nature that anyone should have the sea or the use thereof proper to himself, as we have now sufficiently declared. To conclude, therefore: seeing the Pope cannot take any man's right from him, what defense shall this fact have if

---

1. Vitoria, *De Indis,* II. 2.
2. Sylvester Prierias, *Summa Sylvestrina,* on the word *Papa,* XVI.

with one word he should exclude so many people, undeserving, uncondemned and harmless, from that right which no less appertained unto them than to the Spaniards?

Therefore we must either say that such a pronouncing was of no force or, which is no less credible, that the Pope's meaning was such that he desired the strife between the Castilians and the Portugals should be mediated but nothing of others' right diminished.

CHAPTER 7

That the sea or right of sailing is not proper to the Portugals by title of prescription or custom

The last defense of injustice is wont to be in prescription or custom. And the Portugals therefore come thronging hither, but the most certain reason of the law debarreth them of either defense. For prescription is from the civil law, wherefore it can have no place among kings or among free people, much less where the law of nature or nations resisteth it, which always is more forcible than the civil law.[1] But here even the very civil law itself forbiddeth prescription.[2] For those things are forbidden to be gotten by prescription which cannot be accounted in the nature of goods, next those things which at all cannot be possessed nor as it were possessed and whose alienation is prohibited.[3] But all these are truly said of the sea and the use thereof.

And seeing public things—that is to say, appertaining to any people—can be said to be gotten by no possession of time, either by reason of the nature of the thing or by reason of their privilege against whom this prescription should proceed, how much more justly was that benefit to be

1. Vázquez, *Controversiae illustres,* I. 23. 3–4.
2. Doneau, *Commentarii de jure civili,* V. 22 ff.
3. *Digest,* XVIII. 1. 6; *Digest,* XLI. 3. 9, 25; *Sext,* V. 12, ult. reg. 3; *Digest,* L. 16. 28; *Digest,* XXIII. 5. 16.

given in common things to mankind than to one people?[4] And this that which Papinianus hath left in writing, that prescription of long possession to obtain the public place of the law of nations is not wont to be granted. And he giveth an example thereof in a shore, part whereof was possessed by a building set upon it, for that being overthrown and another man's building set up in the same place afterward could not be opposed as an exception, which he illustrateth by a similitude of a public thing.[5] For although any man have fished many years in the creek river, afterwards, the fishing being interrupted, he could not forbid another by the same right.

It is apparent therefore that Angelus and they who with Angelus said that the Venetians and Janueses might get sound right to a bay of their sea lying before their shore were either deceived or deceivers,[6] which is too usual among lawyers, seeing they confer the authority of a holy profession not to reason and laws but to the favor of the more mighty. For surely Marcianus' answer (whereof also we spake before),[7] if it be rightly compared with Papinianus' word, can receive no other interpretation than that which was sometimes allowed of Johannes and Bartolus and is now received of all the learned: to wit, that the right of prohibiting should proceed so long as the occupation continueth, but not if it be omitted.[8] For being omitted it profiteth not, although it had been continued a thousand years, as Castrensis rightly observeth.[9] And although Marcianus would have had it so (which he is not supposed to have thought) that prescription should be granted in the same place where the occupation is granted, yet to apply that which was spoken of a public river to the common sea, and of a creek to a bay, was absurd, seeing this prescription should hinder that use which by the law of nations is common, but that should not much

---

4. *Code*, VIII. 12. 6; *Code*, XI. 42, 9; *Digest*, XLIII. 11. 2.

5. *Digest*, XLI. 3. 45.

6. Angelus, *Consilia,* CCXC. This is the theme in the other chapters on peace [Grotius's note].

7. *Digest*, XLIV. 3. 7.

8. Douaren on *Digest*, XLI. 3; Cujas on *Digest*, XLI. 3. 45; Doneau, *Commentarii de jure civili*, V. 22.

9. Castrensis on *Digest*, XLI. 1. 14, n. 4.

hurt the public use. But the other argument of Angelus, drawn from conduit,[10] by the opinion of the same Castrensis is worthily exploded of all as furthest from the question.[11]

It is false therefore that such a prescription should be created at that time whose beginning might exceed all memory. For where the law taketh away all prescription, this time surely is not admitted; that is to say, as Felinus speaketh, a matter unprescribable is not made prescribable by time out of mind.[12] Balbus confesseth this to be true but saith that the opinion of Angelus was allowed for this reason: because time out of mind is supposed to be of the same validity that privilege is, seeing the best title may be presumed to be drawn from such a time.[13] Hereby it appeareth that they meant nothing else than if any part of a commonwealth (as, for example, the empire of Rome) beyond all memory had used such a right, by this color a prescription was to be given unto it as though the grant of the prince had gone before. Wherefore, seeing no man may be lord of all mankind who might grant that right to any man or people against all men, that color being taken away it is necessary also that prescription should be overthrown. And so also by their opinion the course of infinite time among kings or free people can nothing avail.

But that also is most vain or foolish which Angelus taught: although prescription cannot profit for dominion yet an exception was to be given to the possessor. For Papinian in plain words denieth the exception.[14] And he could not think otherwise, seeing in his time prescription was nothing else but exception. It is true, therefore, which the Spanish laws express:[15] in those things which are attributed to the common use of men, no prescription of time at all can proceed, of which definition that reason before the rest may begin, that who so useth a common thing seemeth to use it

---

10. *quod ex aquaeductu sumitur:* referring to *Code,* XI. 41, "Concerning aqueducts."
11. Angelus on *Code,* XI. 42. 4, 9; *Digest,* XLIII. 20. 3, 4.
12. Felinus on *Decretals,* II. 26. 11.
13. Balbus, *De praescriptionibus,* V. 4, q. 6, n. 8.
14. *Digest,* XLI. 3. 45.
15. *Las Siete Partidas,* Pt. III, tit. 29, law 7; Suárez, *De usu maris,* I. 4.

as common, not in his proper right, and so can no more prescribe than he that taketh the benefit of a thing by the fault of possession.

This other also is not lightly to be regarded: that in prescription of time out of mind, although title and plain dealing may be presumed, yet if it appear indeed that no title may be given and so the deceit be manifest (which specially in the people, as in one body, is thought to be perpetual), the prescription faileth by reason of the double effect.[16] But the third reason is because this thing is of mere faculty, whereof there is no prescription, as we will show hereafter.

But there is no end of subtle arguments. There are some found who in this argument would distinguish custom from prescription, that being excluded from that they might fly unto this. But the difference they make herein is ridiculous. They say that by prescription the right which is taken from one is applied unto another, but when any right is so applied to any that it be not taken away from another, then it is called custom.[17] As if when the right of navigation (which commonly appertaineth unto all) is usurped of one, excluding others, it is not necessary that so much as cometh unto one should be lost unto all.[18] The words of Paulus not rightly understood gave occasion to this error, who, when he spake of the proper right of the sea appertaining to any, Accursius said it might to be done by privilege or custom, which additament no way agreeing with the text of the lawyer seemeth rather to be the addition of an evil conjecturer than a good interpreter.[19] The meaning of Paulus is before declared. But if they had advisedly considered but the very words of Ulpian which go a little before they would have said far otherwise.[20] For he confesseth it was a usual thing to forbid any to fish before my house—that is to say, received by custom but by no right—and therefore an action of trespass was not to be denied him who was forbidden.[21]

---

16. Fachineus, *Controversiarum juris libri tredecim*, VIII. 26, 28; Covarruvias, on *Sext*, rule *de praesc.*, Pt. II, ss. 2, n. 8; ss. 7, nn. 5, 6.

17. Angelus on *Digest*, I. 8; Balbus, *De praescriptionibus*, V. 4, q. 6, n. 2.

18. Vázquez, *Controversiae illustres*, I. 30. 38.

19. Accursius on *Digest*, XLVII. 10. 14.

20. *Digest*, XLVII. 10. 13, § 7.

21. Glossators on *Digest*, XLVII. 10. 13, § 7.

He therefore contemneth this custom and calleth it usurpation, as also Ambrose doth amongst the Christian doctors.[22] And worthily. For what is more clear than that such a custom should not be of force which is opposed clean contrary to the law of nature or the law of nations?[23] For custom is a kind of positive law which cannot derogate from the perpetual law. But that law is perpetual that the sea should be common in use unto all. But what we said in prescription, the same is true in custom; if any man examine the meaning of them who have delivered the contrary, he shall find no other thing but that custom is equivalent to privilege. But no man hath power to grant a privilege against mankind. Wherefore between divers commonwealths this custom hath no force.

But Vasquius, the honor of Spain, hath most carefully handled all this question, whose subtlety in sifting the law and liberty in teaching you would never look for.[24] He, therefore, setting down the question that public places and such as are common by the law of nations cannot be prescribed, confirmeth it by many authorities and after addeth the exceptions framed by Angelus and others which we have before recited. And being about to examine these things, he rightly judgeth that the truth thereof dependeth as well upon the true knowledge of the law of nature as of the law of nations. For seeing the law of nature proceedeth from the divine providence, it is immutable. But part of this natural law is the law of nations, which is said to be that of the first age, diverse from the secondary or positive law of nations, whereof the latter may be changed. For if any customs be contrary to the ancient laws of nations, those be not human (thyself being judge) but brutish corruption and abuses not laws and customs. Therefore they could be prescribed by no time, justified by no law, nor be established, although it were by the consent, entertainment or exercise of many nations, which he confirmeth by some examples and the testimony of Alphonsus Castrensis the Spanish divine:[25]

---

22. Ambrose, *De officiis ministrorum*, I. 28. 132; Gentili, *De jure belli*, I. 19.
23. Leo, *Novellae*, IX; *Decretals*, I. 4. II.
24. Vázquez, *Controversiae illustres*, II. 89. 12–28.
25. Alfonso de Castro, *De potestate legis poenalis*, II. 14.

By the which it appeareth (saith he) how much their opinion, of whom we spoke before, is to be suspected who think the Genoese or also the Venetians might lawfully prohibit others to sail through the gulf of their sea, as if they would prescribe for the sea itself, which is not only against the laws but also against the law of nature itself or the ancient law of nations which, as we have said, cannot be changed.[26] That it is against that law it is manifest, because not only the sea or air by that law were common, but also all things else that were immovable. And albeit in part they afterward varied from that law, to wit, as concerning dominion and property of countries, the dominion whereof by nature being common was distinguished and divided, and so there was a separation from that community.[27] Yet it was and is differing in the dominion of the sea which from the beginning of the world even to this day and always hath been in common, in no part changed, as is well known.

And although I have often heard a great multitude of the Portugals to be of this opinion that their king hath so prescribed for navigation of the West Indian (peradventure the East), yea and that a most huge sea, that it should not be lawful for other nations to cross those seas,[28] and among our Spanish nation the common sort seem almost to be of the same opinion that it should not be lawful for others save only the Spaniards to sail through that huge and vast sea to the Indies which our most puissant kings have conquered, as if they prescribed for that right. Yet all these men's opinions are no less foolish than theirs who, as touching the Genoese and Venetians, are wont to be in the same dream, which opinions that they are fond appeareth more clearly even by this, that every one of these nations cannot prescribe against themselves. That is to say, the commonwealth of the Venetians cannot prescribe against itself, nor the commonwealth of the Genoese against itself, nor the kingdom of Spain against itself, nor the kingdom of Portugal against itself. For there ought to be a difference between the agent and the patient.[29]

---

26. *Digest*, XLI. 1. 14; *Digest*, XLI. 3. 45; *Institutes*, II. 1. 2; *Digest*, XLIV. 3. 7; *Digest*, XLVII. 10. 14.

27. *Digest*, I. 1. 5; *Institutes*, I. 2, § 2.

28. *Digest*, XLI. 3. 4, § 27.

29. *Digest*, XLI. 3. 4, § 27; *Digest*, XXX. 1. 11; *Institutes*, IV. 6. 14; Bartolus on *Digest*, XXX. 1; Jason on *Digest*, XXX. 1.

But against other nations they can prescribe much less because the right of prescription is mere civil, as we have before declared at large. Therefore, such a right ceaseth when the case is between princes or people not acknowledging a superior in temporal things. For laws which are mere civil, of what country soever, as touching foreign people, nations, or particular men, are no more in consideration than if indeed there were no such law or never had been, and we must have recourse to the ancient common or secondary law of nations and are to use the same, by which law it is sufficiently known that such prescription and usurpation of the sea was not admitted. It maketh for our purpose, for even at this day the use of waters is common no otherwise than it was from the beginning of the world. Therefore in the seas and waters no other right can be to mankind than for the common use. Moreover, by law natural and divine it is commanded that thou do not that to another which thou would desire not have done to thee. Whereupon, seeing navigation can be hurtful to none but to him that saileth, it is meet that none either ought or can be barred, lest in a thing which is free by nature and nothing at all hurtful unto him he hinder or hurt the liberty of such as sail contrary to the said precept and contrary to the rule, especially seeing all things are understood to be permitted which are not found expressly forbidden.[30] Furthermore, it should not only be against the law natural to be willing to hinder such navigation, but also we are bound to do the contrary: to wit, to profit those whom we may when it may be done without our damage.[31]

Which, when he had confirmed by many divine and human authorities, he added after:[32]

By those things which have been formerly delivered it appeareth also that the opinion of Faber, Angelus, Baldus, and Franciscus Balbus (whom we before recited) is suspected, who thought that common places, by the law of nations although they could not be gotten by prescription yet by custom they might, which is altogether false, and that tradition is a blind

30. *Digest,* I. 5. 4; *Institutes,* I. 3. 1; *Digest,* XLIII. 29. 1–2; *Digest,* XLIV. 5. 1, § 5; *Code,* III. 28. 35, § 1; *Digest,* IV. 6. 28, §§ 1–2.
31. Vázquez, *Controversiae illustres,* II. 89. 30–35.
32. Ibid., II. 89.36.

tradition and of no force and without any light of reason and making a law for words and not for things.[33] For in the examples of the sea of the Spaniards, Portugals, Venetians, Genoese and the rest, it is manifest that such a right of sailing and of forbidding others to sail is no more gained by custom than by prescription. For in both cases, as appeareth, the reason is alike.[34] And because by the laws and reasons before alleged it had been against natural equity nor should procure any benefit but only hurt, and so as by express law they could not be brought in, so also nor by the secret law such as custom is.[35] And it could not be justified by time, but should daily be made worse and more injurious.[36]

After that he showeth that from the first possession of countries, as the right of hunting so the right of fishing in their own river may belong to a people, and after those things are once separated from the ancient community so that they admit a particular application by prescription of that time, the memory of whose beginning is not extant, they may, as it were by the secret grant of the people, be gotten and obtained. But that this cometh to pass by prescription not by custom, because the condition only of the getter should be made the better and the estate of the rest the worse. And when he had reckoned up three things which are required to prescribe a property for fishing in a river, he addeth:[37]

But what for the sea? And therein it is more, that even the concurring of these three things would not suffice to get a right. The reason of the difference of the sea on the one part and the earth and rivers on the other is this: because in that case, as in times past so at this day and always, as well for fishing and for navigation, the ancient law of nations remained entire, nor was it ever separated from the community of men and applied to a particular man or to any. But in the latter case, to wit, in the land or rivers, it was otherwise, as we have now disputed.

But why did the secondary law of nations, as it maketh that separation

33. Contra *Code*, VI. 43. 2.
34. *Digest*, IX. 2. 32.
35. *Decretum*, I. 4. 2; *Digest*, I. 3. 1–2; *Digest*, I. 3. 32–40.
36. *Decretals*, II. 26. 20.
37. Vázquez, *Controversiae illustres*, II. 89. 39–40.

for countries and rivers, cease to do the same in the sea? Answer, because in that case it was expedient it should be so, but in this case it was not expedient. For it is manifest that if many hunt on the land or fish in a river, the forest will soon be without game and the river without fishes, which is not so in the sea. Further, a river is easily emptied by conduit; it is not so in the sea.[38] Therefore in both the reason is not alike.

Nor doth it appertain to the matter which we said before, that the use of waters was common, even of fountains and rivers. For it is understood concerning drinking thereof and the like which lightly, or little or nothing, hurt him who hath the right or dominion of the river. For the least things are not respected in the law.[39] It maketh for our opinions because unjust things can be prescribed by no time and therefore an unjust law is prescribed or justified by no time.[40]

Again, those things which are unprescribable by the disposition of the law should not be prescribed, though by a thousand years, which he maintaineth by innumerable testimonies of doctors.[41]

No man but now seeth that for the intercepting or forestalling of the use of a common thing no usurpation of any time how long soever can profit or avail. Whereunto we must also add that their authority who dissent or disagree can no way be applied to this question, for they speak of the Midland Sea, we of the ocean, they of a gulf, we of the huge sea, which in the manner of occupation differs much.[42] And they to whom they lightly grant prescription, even they possess the shores bordering on the sea, as the Venetians and the Genoese, which even now was plainly proved could in no wise be said of the Portugals.

Nay, but if time could profit anything, as something it may in public things which appertain unto the people, yet those things appear not which are necessarily required. For first all men teach that it is required that he

---

38. *Digest,* XLIII. 13. 1.

39. *Digest,* IV. 1. 4; Vázquez, *De successionum resolutione,* I. 7.

40. Balbus, *De praescriptionibus,* V. 5, q. 11; Glossators on *Decretum,* II. 10. 3. 8; Alfonso de Castro, *De potestate legis poenalis,* II. 14.

41. Vázquez, *Controversiae illustres,* II. 89. 44; Baldus and Angelus on *Code,* VII. 39. 4.

42. Angelus on *Institutes,* II. 1. 5.

who prescribeth for such an act should exercise the same not only a long time but such a time as exceedeth memory; then, that for so long time no man else exercised the same act, but by his grant, though it were secretly;[43] and further that he hath forbid others that would use it, they to whom the matter appertaineth knowing and suffering it. For although he had always exercised it and had always forbid some who would have exercised it yet not all, because some were forbidden but some exercised it freely, that truly was not sufficient by the doctors' opinion.

But it appeareth that all these things must concur, both because the law is an enemy to prescription of public things and also that he which prescribeth may seem to have used his own right and not the common right, and that without interrupting his possession. And seeing such a time is required of whose beginning there is no memory, it is not always sufficient, as the best interpreters declare, to prove that one age is run out.[44] But it ought to be manifest that the fame or report of the thing was delivered over by our elders unto us, so that none remaineth alive who hath seen or heard the contrary.

The Portugals by occasion of the affairs in Africa, in the reign of king John in the year of our Lord God 1477, began first to search into the farthest parts of the ocean. Twenty years after, under king Emmanuel, they sailed beyond the Cape de Bona Esperanza, and long after they came to Malacca and the further islands, unto the which the Hollanders began to sail in anno 1595, doubtless within an hundred years.[45] But now also, forasmuch as the usurpation of others came between in that time, it hath hindered or barred prescription, even against all others. The Castilians from the year 1519 have made the possession of the sea about the Moluccas doubtful to the Portugals. The French also and English, not privily but by open violence, have broke through thither. Besides, the borderers of all the coast of Africa or Asia have every one of them usurped by fishing and sailing part of the sea next unto them never forbidden of the Portugals.

43. Angelus on *Institutes,* II. 1. 38.
44. Covarruvias on *Sext,* rule *possessor,* Pt. II, § 3, n. 6.
45. Osório, *De rebus Emmanuelis,* fols. 15b–16a.

Let us therefore conclude that the Portugals have no right whereby they may forbid any other nation from sailing the ocean to the Indians.

CHAPTER 8

That trading is free by the law of nations among all or between any

If the Portugals say that a certain proper right appertaineth unto them of exercising trade with the Indians they shall be confuted almost by the same arguments. We will briefly repeat them and apply them.

This was brought in by the law of nations that all men should have free liberty of negotiation among themselves which no man could take away.[1] And as this was immediately necessary after distinction of dominion so it may seem to have a more ancient beginning. For Aristotle subtly called μεταβλητικὴν ἀναπλήρωσιν τῆς κατὰ φύσιν αὐταρκείας, that is to say, that what was wanting to nature was supplied by negotiation that everyone conveniently might have enough.[2] It ought therefore to be common by the law of nations not only privatively but also positively or affirmatively, as the Schoolmen say.[3]

That may thus be understood. Nature had given all things to all men, but seeing they were barred from the use of many things whereof man's life standeth in need by reason of the distance of places, it was needful to pass over from place to place. Neither yet was there permutation, but finding other things with others they used them at their pleasure by course. Almost after the same manner they report the Seres do, who, leaving their goods in the wilderness, the bargain is made only by the honesty and conscience of the changers.[4]

1. *Digest,* I. 1. 5; Bartolus on *Digest,* I. 1. 5.
2. Aristotle, *Politics,* I. 3 (1257a 30).
3. Covarruvias on *Sext,* rule *peccatum,* Pt. II, § 8.
4. Pomponius Mela, *De situ orbis,* III. 14.

But so soon as movable things (necessity which was even now declared pointing at it) passed into proper right, permutation was found out, whereby that which is wanting unto one should be supplied of that which is superfluous to another.[5] So Pliny proveth out of Homer that traffic was found out for the maintenance of the life of man.[6] But after that immovable things began to be divided unto lords and owners, community being on all parts taken away made trading necessary, not only between men divided by distance of places but also between neighbors, which that it might more easily proceed money was afterward invented, so called απο του νομου, because it was a civil institution.[7]

The universal reason therefore of all contracts ἡ μεταβλητική was from nature, but some particular means and the price itself ἡ χρηματιστική, from institution,[8] which the ancient interpreters of the law did not sufficiently distinguish, yet all men confess that property of things (at the least of movables) to have proceeded from the primary law of nations and also all contracts whereunto no price is added.[9] The philosophers of τῆς μεταβλητικῆς, which we may call translation, make two kinds, τὴν ἐμπορικὴν καὶ τὴν καπηλικὴν, of the which ἐμπορική, which is as the word itself declareth between nations far distant, by the order of nature is the foremost and is so set down by Plato.[10] Καπηλική seemeth to be same which Aristotle calleth παράστασις, a standing or shop negotiation between citizens. The same Aristotle divideth τὴν ἐμπορικὴν into ναυκληρίαν and φορτηγίαν, whereof the one carrieth merchandise by land, the other by sea.[11] But καπηλική is the baser and contrariwise ἐμπορική the more honest or honorable and that chiefly which concerneth the sea, because it imparteth many things to many.[12]

---

5. *Digest*, XVIII. 1. 1.

6. Pliny, *Natural History*, XXXIII. 1 [Grotius's reference].

7. *Digest*, XVIII. 1. 10; Aristotle, *Nicomachean Ethics*, V. 5. 10 (1133a 20); Aristotle, *Politics*, I. 3. 15 (1257b 10).

8. *Decretum*, I. 1. 7; Aristotle, *Politics*, I. 3. 4 (1253a 16).

9. Castrensis citing Cynus et al., on *Digest*, I. 1. 5, nn. 20, 28.

10. Plato, *Sophist*, 223d; Plato, *Republic*, 371b–c, cit. *Digest*, L. 11. 2.

11. Aristotle, *Politics*, I. 3. 16 (1258b 22–23).

12. Cicero, *De officiis*, I. 52. 150; Aristotle, *Politics*, I. 3. 15 (1257b).

Whereupon Ulpian saith that taking of money for freight of shipping appertaineth to the highest and greatest commonwealth.[13] And that there is not the same use of such as are allowed to buy and sell because according to nature that is altogether necessary. Aristotle saith, ἔστι γὰρ ἡ μετα-βλητικὴ πάντων, ἀρξαμένη τὸ μὲν πρῶτον ἐκ τοῦ κατὰ φύσιν, τῷ τὰ μὲν πλείω, τὰ δὲ ἐλάττω τῶν ἱκανῶν ἔχειν τοὺς ανθρώπους, that is to say, for translation of things began from the beginning from that which is according to nature, when men had partly more than was sufficient and partly less.[14] Seneca saith, "the law of nations warranteth thee to sell that which thou has bought."[15]

Therefore, the liberty of trading is agreeable to the primary law of nations which hath a natural and perpetual cause and therefore cannot be taken away and, if it might, yet could it not but by the consent of all nations, so far off is it that any nation, by any means, may justly hinder two nations that are willing to trade between themselves.

CHAPTER 9

That merchandise or trading with the Indians is not proper to the Portugals by title of possession

Invention or occupation hath not the first place here because the right of buying and selling is no corporal thing which may be apprehended. Nor should it profit the Portugals although they had been the first men which had traffic with the Indians, which, notwithstanding, cannot but be most untrue. For seeing in the beginning people went into divers parts, it is necessary that some should be the first merchants who, notwithstanding (it is most certain), gained no right at all. Wherefore, if any right belonged to

13. *ad summam rempublicam:* "of the greatest public importance"; *Digest,* XIV. 1. 1, § 20.
14. Aristotle, *Politics,* I. 3. 12 (1257a).
15. Seneca, *De beneficiis,* I. 9.

the Portugals that they should only trade with the Indians, by the example of other servitudes it must proceed from some grant either expressed or secret, to wit, from prescription. For otherwise it cannot be.

CHAPTER 10

That trading with the Indians is not proper to the Portugals by title of the Pope's donation

No man granted it unless peradventure the Pope, who could not. For no man can grant that which is none of his own. But the Pope, unless he be temporal lord of the whole world (which wise men deny), cannot say that the universal right also of merchandising is in his authority. But chiefly when the thing is wholly applied unto gain and nothing appertaining to the promoting of spiritual things, without which (as all men confess) the Pope's power ceaseth. Further, if the Pope would give that right only to the Portugals, and would take away the same from other men, he should commit double injury. First, to the Indians who, as they are put out of the Church, were no way subject to the Pope, as we have said. Seeing therefore the Pope could take away nothing from them which was theirs, he could not take away that right which they have of trading with whom they pleased. Next, to all other Christian men and infidels, from whom he could not take that right without cause or their cause not being heard. What, cannot temporal lords indeed in their dominions forbid the liberty of trading, as by reasons and authorities before is declared?

So then this likewise is to be confessed, that no authority of the Pope is of force against the perpetual law of nature and nations whence this liberty took beginning, which shall continue forever.

CHAPTER II

That trading with the Indians is not proper to the Portugals by the right of prescription or custom

Prescription remaineth, or custom, whether you please to call it. But that neither the one nor the other have any force among free nations or princes of divers nations, nor against those things which were brought in by the first original law, we have with Vasquius declared.[1] Wherefore here also that the right of trading should become proper, which receiveth not the nature of property, no time can effect. Therefore neither could this title be, nor yet honest and plain dealing, which when it manifestly ceaseth, prescription according to the canons shall not be called right but injury.

But even that very possession, as it were, of trading seemeth not to have befallen them of any proper right but by the common right which equally appertaineth unto all. As, contrarily, in that other nations neglected to contract with the Indians they are not supposed to have done it for the Portugals' sakes, but because they thought it was expedient for them so to do, which hindereth not that they should be less able (when profit shall persuade) to do that which before they did not. For that is a most certain rule delivered by the doctors that in those things which stand in free will and mere faculty, so that by themselves they work an act of that faculty only and not a new right, a thousand years are nothing worth, neither by title of prescription nor custom, which Vasquius teacheth proceedeth both affirmatively and negatively.[2] For I am neither compelled to do that which I did freely nor to omit that which I did not.

Else what were more absurd than for that we cannot all at all times contract with all, thereby our right of contracting with them hereafter (if need require) should not be preserved? The same Vasquius, and that most aptly, affirmeth that an infinite time cannot effect that anything should rather

---

1. See above, pp. 44–45.
2. Glossators and Bartolus on *Digest,* XLIII. 11. 2; Balbus, *De praescriptionibus,* V. 4, q. 1; Panormitanus on *Decretum,* III. 8. 10; Doctors on *Digest,* XLI. 2. 41; Covarruvias, on *Sext,* rule *possessor,* Pt. II, § 4, n. 6; Vázquez, *Controversiae illustres,* I. 4. 10, 12.

seem to be done by necessity than of free will.[3] The Portugals therefore should procure the coaction, which thing itself, seeing in this it is contrary to the law of nature and hurtful to all mankind, it cannot do right. Again, that coaction or constraint ought to have continued for such a time of whose beginning no memory remaineth.[4] But it is so far from that that scarce an hundred years are run out since all the Indian trade almost was in the power of the Venetians by the passages of Alexandria.[5] And the coaction also ought to be such against which there was no resistance. But the French, the English and others resisted. Nor doth it suffice that some should be compelled but it is required that all should be compelled, seeing that possession of liberty in a common cause is kept even by one man not being compelled. But the Arabians and Sinenses from so many ages past unto this day perpetually traffic with the Indians.

Therefore, this their usurpation profiteth nothing.

CHAPTER 12

That the Portugals incline not to equity in forbidding trade

By those things which have been spoken, their blind covetousness sufficiently appeareth who, that they may admit none to take part of the gain, go about to pacify their consciences with those reasons which the Spanish doctors (who are in the same cause) convince of manifest vanity.[1] For they sufficiently declare all those colors which are used in Indian affairs to be unjustly taken and add further that it was never approved by the serious and diligent examination of the divines. But what is more unjust than that

---

3. Vázquez, *Controversiae illustres,* I. 4. 12.
4. Ibid., 11.
5. Guicciardini, *Storia d'Italia,* XIX.
1. Vázquez, *Controversiae illustres,* I. 10. 10; Vitoria, *De Indis,* I. 3.

complaint that the Portugals say their gains are consumed and spent through the multitude of those who are licensed to the contrary? For among the positions of the laws this is most certain, that he who useth his own right is not guilty of deceit nor dealeth fraudulently, much less seemeth to endamage another, which is most true if anything be done with a purpose to increase his own estate not to hurt another.[2] For that which is principally done ought to be looked into, not that which outwardly cometh in consequence.[3] Nay, if we speak properly with Ulpian, he doth not prejudice any, but hindereth him from that gain which yet another used.[4]

But it is natural and agreeable to the highest law and also to equity itself that every man should rather propound his own gain unto himself than another, although his gain who took it before.[5] Who could endure a craftsman complaining that another by exercising the same trade overthrew his commodity? But the Hollanders' cause is so much the more just because their profit in this behalf is joined with the benefit of all mankind which the Portugals go about to overthrow. Nor shall this rightly be said to be done for envy or emulation, as in the like matter Vasquius declareth,[6] for either this is plainly to be denied or we must say it is done not only for a good but also for the best kind of emulation, according to Hesiodus, ἀγαθὴ δ' ἔρις ἥδε βροτοῖσιν: "This is a good contention among men." For, saith he, if any moved with pity should sell corn cheaper in a great dearth, the wicked cruelty of such should be hindered who in the extremity of penury would sell theirs dearer. "It is true," saith he, "that by such means other men's revenues are diminished, nor do we deny it, but they are diminished with the benefit of all. And I would to God the revenues of all the princes and tyrants of the world were so diminished!"[7]

---

2. *Digest*, VI. 1. 27, § 4; *Digest*, L. 17. 55; *Digest*, XLII. 8. 13; *Digest*, XXXIX. 2. 24, § 12; Bartolus on *Digest*, XLIII. 12. 2, n. 5; Castrensis on *Code*, III. 34. 10; *Digest*, XXXIX. 3. 1, § 23.

3. Vázquez, *Controversiae illustres*, I. 4. 3–5.

4. *Digest*, XXXIX. 2. 26.

5. Vázquez, *Controversiae illustres*, I. 4. 3.

6. Ibid., I. 4.5.

7. Hesiod, *Works and Days*, 24.

What, therefore, may seem so unjust as that the Spaniards should have the whole world tributary, so that they might neither buy nor sell but at their pleasure? We hate and also punish engrossers of corn or other commodities in all cities.[8] Nor doth any trade of life seem so wicked and hateful as this engrossing of corn. And that worthily too. For they do injury to nature which is plentiful and liberal to all in common.[9] Nor is to be thought that negotiation was found out for a few men's uses, but to the end that what was wanting unto one should be recompensed through the plenty of another yet with a just advantage or profit propounded unto all who should undertake the danger and labor of transporting.[10]

That very thing therefore which in a commonwealth, to wit, in a less assembly of men, is judged and esteemed grievous and dangerous, is it tolerable in that great society of mankind that the Spanish people should make a monopoly of the whole world? Ambrose inveigheth against them that shut up the seas,[11] Augustine those that stop trading,[12] Nazianzene against co-emptors and suppressors of merchandise who only make a gain by other men's wants and as he most eloquently speaketh, καταπραγμα-τεύονται τῆς ἐνδείας, make a gain of scarcity. Moreover, also by the opinion of that divine wise man, he is publicly bequeathed to the devil and counted accursed who, suppressing sustenance, enhanceth the price of victuals: ὁ συνέχων σῖτον δημοκατάρατος.[13]

Let the Portugals therefore exclaim as much and as long as they list, "Ye take away our gain!" The Hollanders will answer, "Nay, we are careful of our own. Are you angry at this, that we take part with the winds and sea? But who hath promised those gains shall remain yours? It is well with you wherewith we are contented."

8. *Code*, IV. 59. 1.
9. Cajetan on Aquinas, *Summa theologiae*, IIaIIae, q. 77, a. 1.
10. Aristotle, *Politics*, I. 3 (1257a).
11. Ambrose, *Hexaemeron*, V. 10.
12. Augustine, *Questions on Heptateuch*, IV, qu. 44, cit. *Decretum*, II. 23. 2. 3.
13. Gregory Nazianzenus, *Orations*, XLIII, § 34.

CHAPTER 13

That the right of the Indian trade is to be retained and maintained both by peace, truce and war

Wherefore seeing both law and equity required that the trade of India should be free for us as for any other, it remaineth that we wholly maintain that liberty which we have by nature, whether we have peace, truce or war with the Spaniard. For, as touching peace, it is well known it is of two kinds. For it is entertained either upon equal or unequal conditions. The Grecians call that συνθήκην ἐξ ἴσου, this σπονδὰς ἐξ ἐπιταγμάτων, that appertaineth to men, this to servile dispositions;[1] Demosthenes in his oration concerning the liberty of the Rhodians, καί τοι χρὴ τοὺς βουλομένους ελευθερους εἶναι τὰς ἐκ τῶν ἐπιταγμάτων συνθήκας φεύγειν, ὡς ἐγγὺς δουλείας οὔσας: "it behooveth all those that will be free to avoid all conditions whereon laws are imposed as those which are next to servitude."[2] But all conditions are such whereby the one party is abridged in his right, according to the definition of Isocrates who called προστάγματα τὰ τοὺς ἑτέρους ἐλαττοῦντα παρὰ τὸ δίκαιον.[3] For if, as Cicero saith, wars are to be undertaken for that cause that we may live peaceably without injury,[4] it followeth by the same author that peace is not to be called a covenant of slavery but a quiet liberty, seeing that in the judgment of very many, both philosophers and divines, peace and justice differ rather in name than in deed and that peace is not any agreement whatsoever but a well ordered and disposed concord.[5]

But if truce be made it appeareth sufficiently by the nature itself of truces that the condition of any should not in the meantime be made the worse, seeing they may obtain an action in the nature of an interdiction of *uti possidetis*.

1. Thucydides, Isocrates, Andocides [Grotius's note].
2. Isocrates, *Archidamos*, 51.
3. Isocrates, *Panegyricus*, 176.
4. Cicero, *De officiis*, I. 11. 35.
5. Stobaeus, *Florilegium*, IX. 54; Clement of Alexandria, *Stromata*, IV. 6; Augustine, *City of God*, XV. 4.

But if we be violently compelled to war through the unjust dealing of the enemies, the equity of our cause ought to give hope and assurance unto us of good success. For ὑπὲρ μὲν ὧν ἄν ἐλαττῶνται μέχρι δυνατοῦ πάντες πολέμουσι, περὶ δὲ τοῦ πλεονέκτειν οὐχ οὕτως: "For those things wherein all men are injured, all men may fight for them as much as they can. But for the greedy desire of that which is another's they may not do so."[6] Which also Alexander the emperor hath thus expressed, τὸ μὲν ἄρχειν ἀδικῶν ἔργων οὐκ ἀγνώμονα ἔχει τὴν πρόκλησιν, τὸ δὲ τοὺς ὀχλοῦντας ἀποσείεσθαι ἔκ τε τῆς ἀγαθῆς συνειδηρεῶς ἔχει τὸ θαρραλέον, καὶ ἐκ τοῦ μὴ ἀδίκειν ἀλλ᾽ ἀμύνασθαι ὑπάρχει τὸ εὔελπι: "His provocation from whom the injury began is most spiteful. But when robbers and murderers are discomfited, as a good conscience bringeth boldness and assurance with it, so because we go about to revenge and not to do a wrong it giveth occasion to hope well."[7]

If it must needs be so, proceed, thou most invincible nation on the sea, and boldly fight not only for thine own liberty but for the freedom and liberty of all mankind!

> nec te, quod classis centenis remigat alis
> terreat (invito labitur illa mari)
> quodve vehunt prorae Centaurica saxa minantes,
> tigna cava et pictos experiere metus.
> frangit et attollit vires in milite causa,
> quae nisi justa subest, excudit arma pudor.[8]

If many, and even Augustus [sc. Augustine] himself,[9] have thought that arms might justly be taken for that cause by reason a harmless passage was denied through other men's countries, how much more just shall those arms be whereby the common and harmless use of the sea is required,

---

6. Demosthenes, *De libertate Rhodiorum*, 10.

7. Source unknown: not in Plutarch, *Alexander*.

8. "Nor let it frighten you that their fleet is winged, each ship with a hundred oars. The sea on which it sails is unwilling. And though the prows bear figures threatening to throw rocks like the centaurs, you will find them only hollow planks and painted terrors. The soldier's cause makes or mars his strength; if the cause is not just, shame strikes his weapons": Propertius, *Elegies*, IV. 6. 47–52.

9. Augustine, *Questions on Heptateuch*, IV, qu. 44.

which by the law of nature is common unto all? If those nations were justly assailed who in their own land forbid trading unto others, what shall become of those who by violence withhold people which appertain not unto them and restrain their mutual meetings? If this thing were judicially disputed that sentence which should be expected from a good man could not be doubted of. Praetor saith, "I forbid any violence to be done whereby it should not be lawful to convey a ship or a raft in a public river or whereby men might not unlade upon the shore."[10] The interpreters teach that an interdiction is to be granted after the same form for the sea and the shore by the example of Labeo who, when Praetor interdicted, "That you should not do anything in a public river or shore thereof whereby the road or way for ships should be made worse," said the like interdiction laid for the sea: "That you do nothing in the sea or shore whereby any haven, road, or way for ships should be the worse."[11]

Nay, and that after prohibition if any were forbidden to sail on the sea or not permitted to sell his goods or use that which was his own, for that cause Ulpian answered he might have an action of trespass.[12] Moreover, the divines and such as have to do with cases (as they call them) of conscience with one consent deliver that he who hindereth another to buy or sell or preferreth his proper commodity before the public and common benefit, or any way hindereth another in that which appertaineth to the common right, is bound to make restitution of all the loss by the arbitrement of a good man.

According to these things, therefore, a good man judging it would adjudge liberty of merchandise unto the Hollanders and would forbid the Portugals and others who hinder that liberty to do any violence, and would command them to restore their losses. But that which should be obtained in judgment, where justice could not be had by just war should be revenged. Augustine saith, "the unjust dealing of the adverse party procureth just war."[13] And Cicero: "Seeing there are two kinds of striving, the

10. *Digest,* XLIII. 14. 1.
11. *Digest,* XLIII. 12. 1, § 17.
12. *Digest,* XLIII. 8. 2, § 9.
13. Augustine, *City of God,* IV. 15.

one by debating, the other by violence, we must fly to the latter if we cannot use the former."[14] And King Theodoricus: "We are then compelled to arms when justice findeth no place with the adversary."[15] And that which is nearer to our argument, Pomponius answered that he who would usurp a thing common to all with the discommodity of the rest was to be resisted by a strong hand.[16] The divines also teach that as war is rightly undertaken for the defense of everyone's goods,[17] so is it no less rightly undertaken for the use of those things which by the law of nature ought to be common. Wherefore he that shall stop the passage and hinder the carrying out of merchandise may be resisted by way of fact, as they say, even without expecting any public authority.

Which being so, it is not to be feared either that God will not prosper their endeavors who violate the undoubted law of nature instituted by him, or that men themselves would suffer those multitudes who for the only respect of their own gain oppose themselves against the common benefit of mankind.

Finis

Soli Deo Laus et Gloria

14. Cicero, *De officiis*, I. II. 34.
15. Cassiodorus, *Variae*, III. I.
16. *Digest*, XLI. I. 50.
17. Heinrich von Gorkum, *De bello justo*, prop. IX.

Seeing about this time very many of the king of Spain's letters came to our hands, wherein his and the Portugals' purpose is manifestly discovered, I thought it needful of those (whereof there were many of the same argument) to translate two of them into the Latin tongue.

Beloved Viceroy, Signior Martin Alphonsus de Castro,

I the king heartily salute you. A printed copy of the edict which I caused to be made shall come to your hands with these letters, wherein for these reasons which you shall see expressed and others expedient for my affairs I forbid all trade of strangers in the parts of India and other countries beyond the seas. Seeing this thing may be of moment and greatest use, and which ought to be effected with greatest care, I command you that so soon as you shall receive these letters and the edict you would procure the publication thereof with all diligence to be made in all parts and places of this empire, and that you execute that which is contained in the edict without exception of any person of what quality, age or condition soever he be and that without all delay or excuse, and that you proceed to the fulfilling of the commandment by way of mere execution, admitting no impediment, appeal, or grievance to the contrary of whatsoever matter, kind, or quality.

I therefore command this to be fulfilled by those ministers unto whom execution appertaineth, and that it be signified unto them who shall do the contrary that they shall not only do me ill service, but also that I will punish the same parties by depriving them of the offices wherein they serve me. And because it is reported unto me that many strangers of divers nations, Italians, French, Germans, and Low-Country men, remain in those parts, the greater part whereof (as far as we understand) came thither by Persia, and the Turks' kingdom, and not many by this kingdom. Against whom if according to the prescript form and rigor of this edict we proceed, many difficulties may follow thereupon if they fly to the Moors our enemies and show to the bordering neighbors the ordering of my munition and declare the means whereby they may prejudice my estate. I will that you execute this edict as the matter and time will permit and use that wisdom whereby these difficulties may be avoided by providing that you may have all the strangers in your power and keep them according to every man's quality, so that they may be able to attempt nothing against our empire and that I may wholly obtain that end which I have propounded unto myself by this edict.

Written at Lisbon, 28 of November, anno 1606. It was signed under "Rex"; the superscription, "For the king: to Signior Martin Alphonso de Castro his Councillor, and Viceroy of India."[1]

Beloved Viceroy, I the King heartily salute you.

Although I am assured that by your presence and those forces wherewith you went into the southern parts the Hollanders our rebels who remain there and also the inhabitants of the country who gave them entertainment shall be so chastised that neither the one nor the other dare hereafter attempt any such thing, yet notwithstanding it shall be expedient for our safety that you leave a convenient fleet fit for that purpose in these parts of the sea when you shall returne to Goa, and that you commit the command and chief managing thereof to Andreas Furtado Mendosa or if you shall judge any other fitter for that place, as I trust for your dutiful affection towards me you will respect no other thing in that matter than what shall be most profitable for my affairs.

Written at Madrid, 27 January 1607. Signed "Rex"; the superscription, "For the king: to Signior Martin Alphonsus de Castro, his Councillor and Viceroy of India."[2]

1. Philip III to Martin Afonso de Castro, 28 November 1606, in *Documentos remettidos da India,* I, 47–48.
2. Philip III to Martin Afonso de Castro, 27 January 1607, in *Documentos remettidos da India,* I, 134–35.

William Welwod's Critique

"Of the Community and Propriety
of the Seas"

Having of late seen and perused a very learned but subtle treatise (*incerto authore*) entitled *Mare Liberum,* containing in effect a plain proclamation of a liberty common for all of all nations to fish indifferently on all kind of seas, and consequently a turning of undoubted proprieties to a community, as the fifth chapter thereof at large discovers (wherein the unknown author protesteth that he may for his warrant use the authority and words of such old writers as have been esteemed most mighty in the understanding and judging upon the natural condition of things here below), and the discourse being covered with the maintenance of a liberty to sail to the Indians, I thought always expedient by occasion of this argument of fishing contained in my former title,[1] by God's grace to occur thereunto, as manifestly direct at least (in my weak sight) tending to the prejudice of my most worthy prince and his subjects, and that not only by arguments derived from the first verity of the nature of things, but also from his own proofs, warrants, and their authors.

And yet before I go any further I cannot pass the author his ridiculous pretence, in both epistle and beginning of his discourse, as for a liberty only to sail on seas: a thing far off from all controversy, at least upon the ocean, specially since passage upon land through all regions Christian is this day so indifferently permitted to all of all nations, even to Turks, Jews, pagans, not being professed enemies; and therefore much less to be restrained on sea in all respects, so that I cannot but persuade both myself and other loyal subjects that the said pretense is but a very pretense, and

---

1. Welwod, *An Abridgement of All Sea-Lawes,* ch. XXVI, "Of Fishers, fishing, and trafiquers therewith."

so much the more to be suspected as a drift against our undoubted right and propriety of fishing on this side the seas.

Now remembering the first ground whereby the author would make *mare liberum* to be a position fortified by the opinions and sayings of some old poets, orators, philosophers, and (wrested) jurisconsults—that land and sea, by the first condition of nature, hath been and should be common to all, and proper to none—against this I mind to use no other reason but a simple and orderly reciting of the words of the Holy Spirit concerning that first condition natural of land and sea from the very beginning: at which time, God having made and so carefully toward man disposed the four elements, two to swim above his head, and two to lie under his feet; that is to say, the earth and water, both wonderfully for that effect ordered to the upmaking of one and a perfect globe, for their more mutual service to man's use. According to this, immediately after the creation God saith to man, "Subdue the earth, and rule over the fish,"[2] which could not be but by a subduing of the waters also.

And again, after the Flood God saith, "Replenish the earth,"[3] and for the better performance hereof God in his justice against the building of Babylon scattered mankind over all the face of the earth;[4] therefore is it that Moses saith, "These are the isles of the nations divided in their lands."[5] So that hereby is evident that things here done are not so naturally too common, sith God, the author of nature, is also as well author of the division as of the composition, and yet howsoever in his justice (as is said) yet in his mercy also and indulgent care for the welfare and peace of mankind. For those are sentences both vulgar and sure, set down by the Roman jurisconsults:[6] *communio parit discordiam. Quod communiter possidetur, vitio naturali negligitur. Habet communio rerum gerendarum difficultatem.*[7]

---

2. Genesis 1:28.
3. Genesis 9:1.
4. Genesis 11:8 (the Tower of Babel).
5. Genesis 10:5.
6. *Digest,* XXVII. 9. 5, § 16; *Digest,* XXVII. 9. 7.
7. "Community of property breeds disagreement. Whatever is owned communally is neglected due to natural viciousness. Community of goods carries with it difficulty of administration"; cf. *Digest,* XXXI. 1. 77, § 20.

Afterward, the earth, by the infinite multiplication of mankind being largely replenished and therefore of necessity thus divided, and things upon the earth not sufficient for the necessaries and desires of man in every region, followed of force the use of trading upon the seas; not only for the ruling of the fish therein, according to the commandment given by the Creator at the beginning, but also for transporting of things necessary for the use of man. For the which, and other causes above mentioned, the waters became divisible and requiring a partition in like manner with the earth, according to that of Baldus: *videmus, de jure gentium, in mare esse regna distincta, sicut in terra arida.*[8]

And thus far have we learned concerning the community and propriety of land and sea by him who is the great Creator and author of all, and therefore of greater authority and understanding than all the Grecian and Roman writers, poets, orators, philosophers, and jurisconsults, whosoever famous, whom the author of *Mare Liberum* protests he may use and lean to without offence.

Now, sith the weakness of this his first and principal ground doth this way appear, let any man judge upon the truth of that which Cicero (his man) sets down—*sunt privata natura nulla*[9]—and likewise of all other his authors their opinions for the fortification of an original community of things.

It followeth to examine the chief warrants of *Mare Liberum*, and to consider how far they may bear forth to a common liberty for fishing on all seas indifferently.

The author cites Ulpian, a renowned jurisconsult indeed, and Marcian their sentences,[10] alleging that Ulpian should say, *ante aedes meas aut praetorium ut piscari aliquem prohibeam, usurpatum quidem est, sed nullo jure, adeo ut contempta ea usurpatione, injuriarum agere potest. sz. prohibitus.*[11] That is to say, if I should forbid any man to fish before my house, he may

---

8. "We see that, by the law of nations, the sea is divided into distinct realms, like the dry land": Baldus on *Digest,* I. 8. 2, § 1.

9. "There are no things private by nature": Cicero, *De officiis,* I. 7. 21.

10. Grotius, *The Free Sea,* p. 29, above.

11. *Digest,* XLVII. 10. 13, § 7.

misknow such an usurpation and intend action of injury against me for a wrongful staying him from fishing there.

But as I read, Ulpian his words are thus: *sunt qui putant injuriarum me agere posse;*[12] that is, there are men who think, I may intend action, etc. It is true also that Marcian saith, *nemo ad littus piscandi causa accedere prohibetur.*[13] And yet neither of these two jurisconsults pronounceth absolutely in these cases, but upon another higher warrant; and therefore Ulpian adds, *saepissime rescriptum est nec piscari, etc. prohibere posse;*[14] that is, it is by writ most often answered, etc. Which Marcian expounds most clearly when he saith, *nemo igitur ad littus maris piscandi causa accedere prohibetur,* and subjoins his warrant, *idque Divus Pius piscatoribus Formianis rescripsit;*[15] that is, no man is forbidden to come to the seaside and fish, as the emperor Divus Pius did write to the fishers of Formian. So that you see the emperors to have been warrants to these lawyers and their written opinions concerning the voyage of the sea.

Now, to pass the propriety which hereby we see these emperors did claim on the seas, I ask first, to whom did the emperors write such resolutions? Was it not to the professed subjects of their own empire? And what? Even the usage of the seas and coasts of their empire to be indifferently common to every one of their own subjects. And how? *Jure gentium,* that is, according to the law kept by all other nations, to every one of their own nation in like cases.

Moreover, albeit these and other Roman lawyers pronounce so concerning the community of the sea-shore and coast that private men may build houses within the flood-mark and appropriate them to themselves, according to that which Neratius writes, *quod in littore quis aedificat, eius fit:*[16] that is, what a man builds on shore, it becometh his own; yet upon this condition, *tamen decretum praetoris adhibendum est ut id facere liceat,* saith Pomponius:[17] that is, providing the praetor his decree be interponed

---

12. *Digest,* XLVII. 10. 13, § 7.
13. "No-one is forbidden to come to the sea-shore to fish": *Digest,* I. 8. 2, § 4.
14. *Digest,* XLVII. 10. 13, § 7.
15. *Digest,* I. 8. 4.
16. *Digest,* XLI. 1. 14.
17. *Digest,* XLI. 1. 50.

thereunto, or that the prince give grant, as Ulpian writes: *vel ut princeps concedat.*[18] As for the remnant of these sorts of warrants alleged for *mare liberum,* sith they sing all one song for the common use to the people and propriety to the prince, if men will but only mark them, I need not stay further upon them. So that every man may see both the use of the word *commune* and the meaning of *jure gentium* among these lawyers, whereupon this *mare liberum* appears so to be founded that it cannot be shaken. For *commune* there is nothing else but *publicum, quasi populicum,* signifying a thing common for the usage of any of one sort of people and not for all of all nations, according to that of Modestinus: *Roma communis patria est.*[19]

Neither yet doth that word *jure gentium* mean any law set down by common consent of all nations, but only notes the example of the law or custom of other nations, as if they would say the liberty of fishing on our seas and of other doing there and at shore should be common to everyone of the Roman Empire, like as the same is common to all of all other nations on their seas and their shores.

Likewise, that of Placentinus: *quod mare sit in nullius bonis, nisi solius dei;* that is, God is only lord of the sea.[20] And so say we with king David, that the land also is the Lord's.[21] But that of Faber, *mare esse in primavo jure quo omnia erant communia,*[22] I need no otherwise to refute now than I have done above already.

And these are the authors and warrants whereupon *Mare Liberum* infers his conclusion: *demonstratum igitur nec populo, nec privato jus aliquod in mare competere posse, quum occupationem, nec natura, nec publici usus ratio permittat.*[23] Which, how it followeth upon the premises, let men judge,

---

18. *Digest,* XLIII. 24. 3, § 4.
19. "Rome is the common *patria* of us all": *Digest,* L. 1. 33.
20. Placentinus on *Institutes,* II. 1. 1.
21. Psalm 24:1.
22. "The sea has been left in its primeval right, wherein all things were common": Faber on *Institutes,* II. 1. 5.
23. "It hath been declared that neither the people nor any private man can have any property in the sea (for we excepted a creek), seeing neither the consideration of public use nor nature permitted occupation": Grotius, *The Free Sea,* p. 32, above.

sith neither these his authors make for him neither yet the reason inserted in the conclusion bears out, which is, *quum occupationem nec natura, nec publici usus ratio permittat;* that is, neither nature nor the common need suffers the sea to be acquired in property to any occupation.

For answer, first concerning the nature of the sea, as supposed impossibly occupable or acquirable: is this so thought because the sea is not so solid as is the land that men may trade thereon as upon land? Or that it is continually flowing to and fro? Surely, that lack of solidity for man his trading thereon by foot shall not hinder the solid possession of it, far less the occupation and acquiring, if we will give to the sea that which the jurisconsults indulgently grant to the land, which also cannot be denied. Paulus the jurisconsult saith, *qui fundum possidere velit, non utique omnes glebas eius circumambulet, sed sufficit quamlibet parte eius introire, dum mente et cogitatione hac sit ut totum possidere velit usque ad terminum;*[24] that is, it is not needful for him who would possess himself in any part of the land to go about and tread over the same but it is sufficient to enter in upon any part thereof with a mind to possess all the rest thereof, even to the due marches. And what can stay this to be done on sea as well as on land? And thus far concerning the solidity.

As for the flowing condition of the sea, howsoever it be liquid, fluid, and unstable in the particles thereof, yet in the whole body it is not so, because it keeps the prescribed bounds strictly enough concerning the chief place and limits thereof.[25]

Which discourse gives us occasion of force to answer to a scoff cast in by the author of *Mare Liberum* concerning the possibility also of marches and limits for the division of the seas: *mundum dividunt,* saith the foresaid author of *Mare Liberum, non ullis limitibus, aut natura, aut manu positis, sed imaginaria quadam linea: quod si recipitur, et geometrae terras, et astronomi coelum nobis eripient:*[26] that is, they divide the world not by any marches put either by nature or by the hand of man but by an imaginary

---

24. *Digest*, XLI. 2. 3, § 1.
25. Psalm 104:9.
26. Grotius, *The Free Sea*, p. 34, above.

or fantastic line, which kind of doing being embraced the geometers may steal away the earth and the astronomers the heavens from us.

It is true that there are not in every part of the sea isles sensible (as Guernsey is to England in the narrow seas) or sands (as the Washes at the west seas of England) nor rocks or other eminent and visible marks above water for the designation of the bounds (or laying out the limits) of the divisible parts thereof; but God, who is both the distributer and first author of the division and distinction of both land and sea, hath given an understanding heart to man for the same effect as well as for all other necessary actions wherein he hath to employ himself, so that to a very wonder God hath diversely informed men by the helps of the compass, counting of courses, sounding, and other ways to find forth and to design *finitum in infinito* so far as is expedient for the certain reach and bounds of seas properly pertaining to any prince or people.

Which bounds Bartolus hardily extends and allows for princes and people at the seaside an hundred miles of sea forth from their coasts at least,[27] and justly, if they exercise a protection and conservacy so far;[28] and this reach is called by the Doctors *districtus maris, et territorium.*[29] It is true Baldus esteemeth *potestatem, jurisdictionem,* and *districtum,* to be all one.[30]

To conclude, then: since Papinian writes *in finalibus quaestionibus vetera monumenta sequenda esse,*[31] what more evident monuments for our King his right in the narrow seas than these isles of Guernsey, etc.? And for the eastern seas direct from Scotland what is more anciently notorious than that covenant twixt Scottish men and Hollanders concerning the length of their approaching toward Scotland by way of fishing?

And thus far through occasion of answering to that alleged impossibility of acquiring the sea by occupation because (as would appear) of the unsolidity thereof for any foot treading. It rests to touch the other cause natural for that other impossibility which may be the continual flux and

27. Bartolus, *Tyberiadis,* p. 56.
28. Bartolus on *Digest,* L. 16. 99.
29. Glossators on *Decretals,* I. 6. 3.
30. Baldus on *Code,* VI. 25. 9.
31. "In questions of boundaries old monuments are to be followed": *Digest,* X. 1. 11.

instability of the sea, in such sort that it would appear not aye to be one and the self same body but daily changeable. For answer, I must remember that which the jurisconsult sets down so prettily:[32] suppose (says he) a certain college of judges, or a legion of soldiers, or the particular parts of a ship, or of a man's body, should so continually and often be changed and altered that none of that first college or legion could be found alive nor yet any part of the ship or body could be so certainly demonstrate that it might be affirmed for the very same that it was at the first; yet if that college or legion be in number full, and the ship or man whole and able in all the frame, they shall be accounted and esteemed not to be new but to be the very same which they were at the beginning. Even so, however the sea many ways and hourly changes in the small parts thereof by the ordinary rush on land, mixture with other waters, swelling in itself, exhalation and back receipts thereof by rain, yet since the great body of the sea most constantly keeps the set place prescribed by the Creator, I see not in this respect neither wherefore the nature of the sea should not yield to occupation and conquest. And thus far concerning *Mare Liberum* his last and great conclusion against all appropriation thereof by people or princes. I call it his last great conclusion because of other two passing before, whereof the first is this: *mare igitur proprium alicuius fieri non potest, quia natura jubet esse commune.*[33] And for what reason? Even because Cicero, Virgil, and Plautus have said so. To whom I could also assent concerning the great, huge, and main body of the sea. His next conclusion is this: *est igitur mare in numero eorum quae in commercio non sunt, hoc est, quae proprii juris fieri non possunt;*[34] that is, the sea to be of that order of things which cannot be appropriate to any man. His warrants for his conclusion also are the Roman lawyers whom I said to be wrested by *Mare Liberum,* and therefore must show the same, contrary to his purpose indeed. Marcianus, as the author of *Mare Liberum* largely grants,[35] saith that if any pri-

---

32. *Digest,* V. 1. 76 (Alfenus).

33. "The sea therefore cannot be altogether proper unto any because nature . . . commandeth it should be common": Grotius, *The Free Sea,* p. 26, above.

34. "The sea therefore is in the number of those things which are not in merchandise and trading, that is to say, which cannot be made proper": Grotius, *The Free Sea,* p. 30, above.

35. Grotius, *The Free Sea,* p. 29, above.

vate man have himself alone by any lawful space of time sufficient for a prescription kept and exercised fishing in any creek or nook of sea, which they call *diverticulum,* he may forbid all others to fish therein,[36] which Papinianus also confirmeth.[37] The which as I accept so I would further demand of him by what reason should a private man, who hath no other care nor respect but to himself alone, be thus privileged and preferred to a prince, who not for himself but for his people also in common, yea, and for the safety of all traders passing his coasts, with great charges and care protects and conserveth the seas nearest unto him? Shall not this prince be acknowledged, at least with the good which that sea conserved by him offers so directly to him? And I pray you say what less authority had Leo than the rest of the Roman emperors to grant to everyone in particular having possessions at the seaside as much of the sea as was nearest against their lands with the fishings thereof?[38] What then, shall not princes be equalled in these cases with subjects? Or, rather, have not all princes a like right and power within their own precinct and bounds as these Roman princes had?

But now to draw nearer to the chief point of our purpose, and so to the end thereof. As I accepted *Mare Liberum* his former large grant, so now also do I more heartily embrace the next, which is this: when after these his conclusions, he had said *in tanto mari siquis piscatu arceret, insanae cupiditatis notam non effugeret,*[39] he subjoins according to that of Cicero, *quando sine detrimento suo quis potest alteri communicare in iis quae sunt occupanti utilia et danti non molesta, quid ni faceret?,*[40] and subjoins afterward: *et si quicquam eorum prohibere posset, puta piscaturam, qua dici quodammodo potest pisces exhauriri;*[41] that is to say, if the uses of the seas may be in any respect forbidden and stayed it should be chiefly for the fishing,

36. *Digest,* XLI. 3. 7.
37. *Digest,* XLI. 3. 45.
38. Leo, *Novellae,* CII, CIII, CIV.
39. "If any in so great a sea . . . should forbid others to fish, he could not escape the brand of the brainsick covetousness": Grotius, *The Free Sea,* p. 33, above.
40. "What else, for when he may without his own damage let him impart unto another in such things as are profitable to the receiver and not offensive to the giver?": Grotius, *The Free Sea,* p. 33, above; Cicero, *De officiis,* I. 16. 51–52.
41. "And if it could forbid any of those things, to wit, fishing, whereby it may be said after a sort that fishes should be taken": Grotius, *The Free Sea,* p. 37, above.

as by which the fishes may be said to be exhaust and wasted, which daily experience these twenty years past and more hath declared to be overtrue. For whereas aforetime the white fishes daily abounded even into all the shores on the eastern coast of Scotland, now forsooth by the near and daily approaching of the buss-fishers the shoals of fishes are broken and so far scattered away from our shores and coasts that no fish now can be found worthy of any pains and travails, to the impoverishing of all the sort of our home fishers and to the great damage of all the nation. Whereby I see at last the author of *Mare Liberum* not so addict to serve any man's particular desires as to answer (forsooth) to his profession of the laws; that is, to allow the proper right for every man and nation and to hurt none, according to the three general precepts of all laws, set down by Gaius[42] and after him by Tribonianus: *honeste vivere; alterum non laedere; et jus suum cuique tribuere,*[43] whereof the second tries and rules the rest, according to the vulgar saying out of Pomponius, *neminem debere cum alterius damno locupletari,*[44] and that of Tryphoni[n]us, *ex aliena jactura lucrum haurire non oportet.*[45] And therefore I would meet him with his deserved courtesy, even to proclaim *mare liberum* also, I mean that part of the main sea or great ocean which is far removed from the just and due bounds above mentioned properly pertaining to the nearest lands of every nation. *Atque ita esto mare vastum liberrimum.*[46]

42. *Institutes,* I. 1. 3.

43. "To live honorably; not to harm another; and to give each their due": *Digest,* I. 1. 10, § 1 [*sc.* Ulpian].

44. "No-one should enrich himself by harm to another": *Digest,* L. 17. 206; *Digest,* XII. 6. 14; *Digest,* XXIII. 3. 6, § 2.

45. "No-one should derive profit from the loss of another": cf. *Digest,* XX. 5. 12, § 1.

46. "And this should be the great and most free sea."

Hugo Grotius's Reply

"Defense of Chapter V of the *Mare Liberum*"

Which had been attacked by William Welwod, Professor of Civil Law, in Chapter XXVII of that book written in English to which he gave the title "An Abridgement of All Sea-Lawes"

A few years ago, when I saw that the commerce with that India which is called East was of great importance for the safety of our country and it was quite clear that this commerce could not be maintained without arms while the Portuguese were opposing it through violence and trickery, I gave my attention to stirring up the minds of our fellow-countrymen to guard bravely what had been felicitously begun, putting before their eyes the justice and equity of the case itself, whence I thought was derived "the confidence" (τὸ εὔελπι) traditional with the ancients. Therefore, the universal laws of war and of prize, and the story of the dire and cruel deeds perpetrated by the Portuguese upon our fellow-countrymen, and many other things pertaining to this subject, I treated in a rather long *Commentary* which up to the present I have refrained from publishing.

But when, a short time thereafter, some hope for peace or truce with our country was extended by the Spaniards, but with an unjust condition demanded by them, namely, that we refrain from commerce with India, a part of that *Commentary,* in which it was shown that this demand rested neither upon law nor upon any probable color of law, I determined to publish separately under the title of *Mare Liberum,* with the intention and hope that I might encourage our countrymen not to withdraw a title from their manifest right and might find out whether it were possible to induce the Spaniards to treat the case a little more leniently, after it had been deprived not only of its strongest argument but also of the authority of their own people. Both of these considerations were not without success. To this little book I had refrained from signing my name, because it seemed to me to be safe, like a painter skulking behind his easel, to find out the judgment of others and to consider more carefully anything that might be published to the contrary. For this purpose I had no idea that I would not have the leisure which is now wanting. In fact, I was expecting that some Spaniard would write a reply to my little book, a thing which I hear was done at Salamanca,[1] but as yet I have not happened to see that book. Meanwhile, a man erudite and much disposed to defending paradoxes, William Welwod, Professor of Civil Law, published at London a book in English entitled *An Abridgement of All Sea-Lawes,* in Chapter XXVII of which he proceeded to attack directly Chapter V of the *Mare Liberum.*

Now the inscription of that Chapter V of my book was as follows: "Neither the Indian Ocean nor the right of navigation thereon belongs to the Portuguese by title of occupation." With this inscription the order and continuity of the entire chapter is clearly in harmony. But, in order to prove what I had had in mind, I had divided the treatment there in such a way as to make clear this sea neither could be occupied nor in fact had been occupied by the Portuguese. To show that it could not have been occupied, I used the following argument. The sea can not become the property of anyone, but owes forever to all men a use which is common to all. To clinch the argument, I cited authorities who asserted that not even fishing on the sea could be prohibited by anyone. This argument had a twofold use. For the cause was demonstrated from the effect, namely, the community of the sea from the freedom of fishing; and the less from the greater, for if fishing should be free, which takes something from the sea, much more would navigation, which takes nothing. This question of fishing, therefore, was not "a general position" (στάσις), but "a special point" (εἰδικόν τι κεφάλαιον), as is apparent to anyone who reads.

But Welwod, a man rather suspicious and who can see what does not

---

1. Justo Seraphim de Freitas, *De justo imperio Lusitano Asiatico.*

exist, tries to persuade himself and others that the intention of the author was to assert the freedom of fishing and that the Indian controversy was used for the attempt.[2] Now the argument which he adduces in support of this suspicion, namely, that it is ridiculous to defend the freedom of navigating the sea because that is not called into question, I do not see how I could more appropriately term than by the use of his word, ridiculous. If there were greater regard for justice and truth than for private interests, surely freedom of navigating the sea would not be called into question, but no more would freedom of fishing be called into question. For in support of the freedom of both is the very excellent testimony of nature and of the jurists.

But we live in an age in which there is nothing so certain that it may not be called into question. Every case finds its patron. So, Welwod attacks the freedom of fishing; others, in spite of Welwod's denial, the freedom of navigation. That the Spaniards claim that freedom of navigation over certain parts of the ocean is prohibited to the other nations is known both to the French and to the British, who have participated in peace negotiations at Vervins and London.[3] The same thing is experienced daily by the sailors of different nations, whom the Spaniard hostilely attacks on the ground that freedom of navigation has been usurped. Finally, the Spanish Senator Vázquez acknowledges it and these are his very words:

And although I have often heard a great multitude of the Portugals to be of this opinion that their king hath so prescribed for navigation of the West Indian (peradventure the East), yea and that a most huge sea, that it should not be lawful for other nations to cross those seas, and among our Spanish nation the common sort seem almost to be of the same opinion that it should not be lawful for others save only the Spaniards to sail through that huge and vast sea to the Indies which our most puissant kings have conquered, as if they prescribed for that right. Yet all these men's opinions are no less foolish than theirs who, as touching the Genoese and Venetians, are wont to be in the same dream.[4]

2. Welwod, "Of the Community and Propriety of the Seas," p. 65, above.
3. Treaty of Vervins (1598); Treaty of London (1604).
4. Vázquez, *Controversiae illustres,* II. 89. 31.

Welwod surely ought not to have said this right has not been called into question by anyone. Because both the Venetians and the Genoese have defended it in word and deed as regards the Mediterranean, and both the Spaniards and the Portuguese as regards the ocean. Much less should he have, upon such a foundation, erected that suspicion, as if one thing were done and another pretended. We now show how the argument drawn from fishing pertains to the question of navigation. This can be made apparent even from Welwod's book itself. For he, in order to destroy freedom of fishing, maintains that the sea can be the property of someone, and this, indeed, necessarily for his purpose. For the use of that which belongs to no one must necessarily be open to all, and among the uses of the sea is fishing. Now he who has conceded that the sea belongs to someone is very easily led to concede likewise that transit over it is not free, after the manner of an estate, entrance to which the owner can forbid to the non-owner.[5]

It is certainly a very powerful argument, for maintaining the freedom of navigation, that the sea belongs to no one. For if anyone tries to say that the sea belongs to someone, but in such a way that it owes to others the servitude of transit, he will easily be refuted by the reply of Ulpian, who said that a servitude can not be imposed upon the sea for the reason that the sea is by nature open to all.[6] Therefore those who, borne from abroad, navigate on the sea, do not do this on another's property by the right of servitude, but on something that is common to all by the right of liberty. No other argument is used by the Emperor Justinian when he says: "And indeed by the natural law these things are common to all: air, running water and the sea, and, therefore, the shore of the sea. No one, therefore, should be prohibited access to the shore of the sea."[7] Here the word "therefore" shows that the cause of free access is the very community of the thing, and when this is removed, it follows that freedom of access also is removed.

Therefore by a certain nexus the right of fishing inheres in the right of navigation, and so Ulpian joins them together as cognate, "may anyone be prohibited from fishing or navigating on the sea?"[8] and says that in both

5. *Institutes,* II. 2, § 12.
6. *Digest,* VIII. 4. 13.
7. *Institutes,* II. 1, § 1.
8. *Digest,* XLIII. 8. 2, § 9.

cases action for damages is competent. Far from that disputation in defense of the community of the sea giving just offense to the British, on the contrary that labor should be especially pleasing to them, seeing that it strongly supports the case of the British against the Spaniards. For no weapon could be more effectively opposed to the Spaniards in their desire to prevent the British and other nations from navigating the Indian Ocean than this: "The sea is common to all; therefore no one should be prohibited access thereto."

Welwod fashions for himself a straw soldier when he says that the foundation of the *Mare Liberum* was determined by himself to be as follows: "Land and sea, by the first condition of nature, hath been and should be common to all, and proper to none."[9] Scarcely anything more foolish could have been said. Far different is the opinion of my little book, as is clear even from that Chapter V itself. For here it is shown that by nature neither land nor sea is the property of anyone, but that land through nature can become property, while the sea can not. A great difference, therefore, is established in this part between land and sea. These are the very words:

> Which being so, all immovable things—to wit, fields—could not remain undivided.[10]

And thereafter:

> Occupation or possession in movables is apprehension; in immovables, instruction and limitation.[11]

And still farther on:

> But occupation is made public after the same manner that it is made private. Seneca saith, "we call those the bounds of the Athenians or Campanians which afterward the borderers divide among themselves by private bounds." For every nation,

---

9. Welwod, "Of the Community and Propriety of the Seas," p. 66, above.
10. Grotius, *The Free Sea,* p. 22, above.
11. Ibid., p. 23, above.

partita fines regna constituit, novas
extruxit urbes.

After this manner Cicero saith, "the territory of the Arpinates is called Arpinatum, of the Tusculans, Tusculanum; the like description," saith he, "is of private possessions, whereupon because every man's own consisteth of those things which by nature were common, let every man hold that which fell to his share." But contrariwise Thucydides calleth that land which fell to no people in division αοριστον, to wit, indefinite.

Of these things which hitherto have been spoken two things may be gathered. The first is that those things which cannot be occupied or were never occupied can be proper to none because all propriety hath his beginning from occupation. The other is that all those things which are so ordained by nature that anyone using them they may nevertheless suffice others whomsoever for the common use are at this day (and perpetually ought to be) of the same condition whereof they were when nature first discovered them.[12]

Soon thereafter come the words:

Of this kind the air is for a double reason, both because it cannot be possessed and also because it oweth a common use to men. And for the same cause the element of the sea is common to all, to wit, so infinite that it cannot be possessed and applied to all uses, whether we respect navigation or fishing.[13]

And some pages later:

The sea therefore is in the number of those things which are not in merchandise and trading, that is to say, which cannot be made proper.[14]

Therefore he who wishes to express properly the opinion of that little book should not lay down the foundation which Welwod fashions for himself, but that which the author himself has expressed only too clearly: "The sea not only was common from its first origin, but also can not become the property of anyone by nature."[15]

12. Grotius, *The Free Sea*, p. 24, above.
13. Ibid., p. 25, above.
14. Ibid., p. 30, above.
15. cf. Grotius, *The Free Sea*, p. 27, above.

This pronouncement of right reason is nowhere opposed by Holy Writ, nor is it out of harmony with those surest of witnesses, nature and Scripture. Welwod first cites what was said by God to Adam and Eve: "You shall have dominion over the fish of the sea and the birds of the air, and all the beasts crawling upon the earth."[16] But this passage has no connection with the question of property, for the ownership which God there confers is universal, not particular, as was properly explained in the *Mare Liberum*. God gave those things not to this person or that person, but to the human race. For Adam and Eve bore the personality of the whole human race, both because they were the only human beings of that time, and because the line of the human race that was to come was contained in those two as the very cause and principle of being. Therefore there is no question there of a right which is competent to men against other men, but of one to all men against the lower creatures. So, in the words that follow, God says that the grasses are granted by Him to the beasts,[17] namely in the same way as He had granted the beasts themselves to man to be used, ordaining all lower things for the use of the higher. Hence it is clear that there is indicated by the divine words "a having and possession" ($\tau\dot{\eta}\nu$ $\check{\epsilon}\zeta\iota\nu$ $\kappa\alpha\grave{\iota}$ $\sigma\chi\acute{\epsilon}\sigma\iota\nu$), which "species" ($\tau\grave{\alpha}$ $\epsilon\check{\iota}\delta\eta$) have "with regard to species" ($\pi\rho\grave{o}s$ $\tau\grave{\alpha}$ $\epsilon\check{\iota}\delta\eta$), not "individuals with regard to individuals" ($\check{\epsilon}\kappa\alpha\sigma\tau\sigma\iota$ $\pi\rho\grave{o}s$ $\check{\epsilon}\kappa\alpha\sigma\tau\alpha$).

But if anyone nevertheless should persist in claiming that there is question here also of the right of occupation by which individuals make individual things their own, not even then does this argument contribute anything to the point. For there is mention there only of living creatures, swimming, flying and crawling; no mention of the sea also. As for Welwod's remark that the fish of the sea could not have been put in subjection unless the waters likewise were put in subjection, if by the word "subjection" he understands that use which the sea owes to the human race in common, we shall have no objection. But if he extends it to mean that the sea, no less than the fish themselves, can become the property of any men, this neither will the words of Scripture nor any reason bear out. For the

---

16. Genesis 1:28.
17. Genesis 1:30.

difference between these is great, and we have shown in the *Mare Liberum* that it was not unknown to Athenaeus and Plautus.[18]

Indeed, that argument is of such slight consequence that it could properly be altered and twisted back against Welwod in the following way. It is licit for anyone to catch fish in the sea, therefore it is clear that the sea belongs to no one. For if the sea belongs to anyone, it would no more be licit for others to catch fish there than it is licit to fish in another's lake or fishpond or to hunt in another's hunting-ground.[19] Just as Ulpian was right then, when he said that he who builds on the sea does not build on his own property, but makes the building his own by the law of nations,[20] so no less right would it be for us to say that one who fishes in the sea does not fish on his own property, but makes the fish his own by the law of nations.

Another passage which Welwod cites as favoring his opinion is from the story of the sons of Noah. "Moses saith, These are the isles of the nations divided in their lands."[21] For the Hebrew word in that passage should more properly be translated "regions" or "provinces" than "islands," since few nations have their abode in islands, while all are distributed into provinces and regions. And what is this but what was in the *Mare Liberum,* that the individual lands were occupied by individual peoples, whence one land was called that of the Arpinates, another of the Tusculans, these the territory of the Athenians, the others of the Campanians?[22]

Moreover, Moses does not say that "the seas" were divided by the nations. Nor if that interpretation please which says that the islands were divided, does it therefore follow that the sea also was divided. For an island is one thing and the sea another. An island is circumscribed by limits, not so the sea. The sea owes a common use, islands do not. Indeed, it is on this very account that an island rising up in the sea becomes the property of the occupier, because the sea belongs to no one. For an island which arises in water that belongs to someone becomes the property of him to whom the water belongs. If the sea were bounded by islands, it might be

18. Grotius, *The Free Sea,* p. 26, above.
19. *Digest,* XLVII. 10. 13, § 7.
20. *Digest,* XXXIX. 1. 1, § 18.
21. Genesis 10:5.
22. Grotius, *The Free Sea,* p. 24, above.

possible to say that the sea was occupied at the same time as the islands were occupied. Now since the islands are in the sea and not the sea in the islands, what sane person will say that the islands could not have been occupied without the sea also being occupied?

There is no reason, therefore, why Welwod boasts of the authority of Holy Writ, in which there is not the least bit of support for his position. There is no reason also why in this attack he should escape the testimony of illustrious authorities in favor of the freedom of the sea. For when we have not the divine words, the next best thing to be considered in a question of the law of nations is, what have the different nations decided from ancient times; and if it is clear that they have held the same opinion, this should be considered as a great argument for truth. For, as Heraclitus rightly said, "the common word is the best criterion, for what seems best to all is trustworthy."[23]

Among these [common opinions] I greatly wonder that that statement of Cicero should be ridiculed, namely, that "there is nothing private by nature,"[24] since it is of most evident truth. For Cicero does not mean thereby that nature is opposed to ownership, and, as it were, forbids anything at all becoming property, but that nature of itself does not cause anything to be property. This can be gathered from the following. Nature produces the rest of things for men, but without distinction, not "this for this one and that for that one." Therefore, in order that this thing become the property of that man, some deed of the man should intervene, and therefore nature itself does not do this by itself. Hence it is evident that community is prior to property. For property does not occur except through occupation, and before occupation, there must precede the right of occupation. Now this right is not competent to this man or that man, but to all men equally, and is rightly expressed under the term "natural community." And hence it happens that what has not yet been occupied by any people or by a man is still common, that is, belongs to no one, and open equally to all. By this argument it is surely proved that nothing belongs to anyone by nature.

23. Stobaeus, *Florilegium,* III. 84.
24. Cicero, *De officiis,* I. 7. 21.

Another argument can be added, namely, that necessity, which reduces everything to the natural law, because the mother of positive law is utility which should yield to necessity, makes common again things formerly owned. By this law, if food becomes scarce on board ship, what each one has is gathered together in a common store.[25] By this law, for the sake of warding off fire, it is licit to cut down neighboring buildings.[26] Many things of this tenor can be seen in Thomas Aquinas and his interpreters.[27]

Add also the fact that eminent theologians are of the opinion that in the primeval state of Paradise there was no property, that is, as distinct from use, and that there would not have been, had not sin intervened. This can be all the more probably defended, because both the Essenes of old and some peoples in America have made use of community of property, which even now a few congregations make use of, and indeed without great inconvenience. By this example it is proved that the statement, which is usually made and is adduced by Welwod, that "what is common is neglected, that community carries with it difficulty of administration, and that discord even arises therefrom,"[28] is not "absolutely necessary," but "a result of hypothesis," since we have taken into consideration the cupidity of men who consult their own interest to the neglect of others. For otherwise, if the human race were of such character as the Christian disciples of the Apostles were in the earliest times, whose hearts and souls were one,[29] why could there not be observed what was then observed, namely, that nothing belong to anyone, but all things be common?

Why is it that today even, although amid such great corruption of morals, still we see many things remaining common, not among private individuals only, but likewise among peoples, and not only for many years, but for centuries? Welwod himself wishes the sea to be common to the citizens of a single people. Consequently, even from this it is apparent that it has not been always and universally true that the disadvantages of community of ownership are greater than the advantages.

25. *Digest,* XIV. 2. 2, § 2.
26. *Digest,* IX. 2. 49, § 1.
27. Aquinas, *Summa Theologiae,* IIaIIae, q. 66, a. 7.
28. Welwod, "Of the Community and Propriety of the Seas," p. 66, above.
29. Acts 4:32.

Nor is it unworthy of mention that, shortly after the creation of the world, when the number of the human race was small and living was simpler, that ownership of individual things which is distinct from use was much less necessary than it is now, than it became afterwards. For a certain necessity of ownership as it were arose from the fact that some things were sufficient for the uses only of a few individuals. Thus we see in arid regions there has been a departure from community of land after competition over wells had arisen. Thus with the increase in the number of cattle, the lands which were common to Abraham and Lot soon began to be divided. Hence you may without rashness gather that, even after sin entered the world, many things remained common, which by degrees, as the human race grew and the desire for luxuries likewise increased, yielded to individual right.

I do not regret having said these things incidentally, in order that it might be evident that those statements, which very estimable authorities have set down with regard to the original community of property, had their origin in truth, whether an inference of reason led them to that conclusion or whether they themselves had transmitted to posterity the story received from their progenitors. Since all these same authorities relate that by degrees the earth was afterwards divided among many owners, while the sea remained perpetually common to all men, rightly should those who contend to the contrary be suspected of novelty, seeing that out of all antiquity they can not adduce even a single supporter of such unheard of doctrine.

Now let us come to the Roman jurists. Since Welwod knew they had great authority also in explaining the law of nations, he preferred to attribute his own opinion to them rather than to ridicule them likewise as he had ridiculed Cicero. Indeed, that nothing might be wanting to his boldness, the very authorities whom with great violence he attempts to draw over struggling and protesting to his side, these he dares to say were distorted by the author of the *Mare Liberum*. But which of the two did violence to them will be easy for him to judge who has both interpretations before his eyes. We affirm that this was their opinion, that the sea remained common to all men. He, however, denies this and says that they intended nothing else than that the seas were common to any citizen whomsoever of a single people and not likewise to other men, likewise that ownership of the sea belonged to him who commanded the land nearest, that is, in a democracy the sea belongs to the people, in a kingdom to the king.[30] Now that these statements are quite foreign to the opinion of the Roman jurists, we make evident by the following arguments.

The first is one which I shall take from the universal term to which no restriction is found to have been added. The emperor says in the *Institutes*, following Marcianus,[31] that the sea is common "to all," and explaining this Theophilus says "common to all men" (κοινὸν πάντων ἀνθρώπων).[32] From this universal assertion both Marcianus and the emperor infer the following universal negative: "No one therefore is prohibited access to the shore of the sea."[33] It would not be licit to do this, if the word "all" did not signify what Theophilus expressed, namely, "all men," for "no one" is beyond controversy the same as "no man." Therefore the following argumentation is valid. The sea and the shore (insofar as it is the approach to the sea) are common to all men, therefore no man is to be deprived of access thereto.

But if you should say, "The sea and the shore are common to all citizens of a single people," it will not be possible therefrom to effect that no one is to be prohibited access, but only no one of the citizens of that people. Add also what Ulpian said, that the sea was by nature open "to all,"[34] and elsewhere that the sea is common to all, and the shores, just as is the air:[35] and Celsus, that the use of the sea is common "to all men,"[36] which phraseology manifestly excludes every exception. For it is one thing to say "all men" and another to say "all citizens." Neratius likewise stated no less absolutely that the shores have come into the dominion "of no one."[37] He

---

30. Welwod, "Of the Community and Propriety of the Seas," p. 69, above.
31. *Institutes,* II. 1, § 1; *Digest,* I. 8. 2, § 1.
32. Theophilus, *Paraphrasis Institutionum,* 209.
33. *Institutes,* II. 1, § 1; *Digest,* I. 8. 4.
34. *Digest,* VIII. 4. 13.
35. *Digest,* XLVII. 10. 13, § 7.
36. *Digest,* XLIII. 8. 3, § 1.
37. *Digest,* XLI. 1. 14.

did not say "of no private citizen," but simply "of no one," therefore neither of people nor prince.

Now whatever is affirmed of the shore is much more to be affirmed of
the sea. For these qualities belong to the sea *per se;* to the shore, on account
of the sea. Hence Justinian said that the sea was common and "therefore"
the shores of the sea,[38] likewise that ownership of the shores is of the same
right as of the sea and the land or sand underneath the sea.[39] But if one
thing is of such and such a character on account of something else, much
more is this something else of that character.

The second argument is the following very strong one, that in the jurists such terms as "to be common to all" and "to be public to the people,"
"are opposed" (ἀντιδιαιρεῖται); therefore these expressions can not have
the same value, which Welwod nevertheless wishes. This is evident from
the *Institutes,* where the emperor first says: "By the natural law some things
are common to all, some things public";[40] then: "By the natural law the
following are common to all: air, running water and the sea, and therefore
the shores of the sea";[41] and then there follows: "But all rivers and ports
are public."[42] Herein should be noted incidentally this "sign of opposi-
tion" (σημεῖον διαιρέσεως). Not otherwise is Theophilus: "By the natural
law the following are common to all men: air, running water, the sea";[43]
thereafter: "But all rivers and ports are public, that is, to the Roman people."[44] But since the rivers belong to any people or to him to whom the
rights of the people have been transferred, how can the sea be assigned under a different head from the rivers unless the community of the sea is of
greater extent? Or how could "common to all" and "public" constitute different species, if they signify one and the same thing? What, therefore, is
"the distinguishing characteristic" (εἰδοποιός) between these "differences"
(διαφορά)? And we must not omit here that passage of Celsus: "The

38. *Institutes,* II. 1. 1, § 1.
39. *Institutes,* II. 1. 1, § 5.
40. *Institutes,* II. 1. 1.
41. *Institutes,* II. 1. 1, § 1.
42. *Institutes,* II. 1. 1, § 2.
43. Theophilus, *Paraphrasis Institutionum,* 209.
44. Ibid., 210.

shores over which the Roman people have sovereignty (*imperium*), I think, belong to the Roman people, but the use of the sea is common to all men."[45] Manifestly he opposes to one another those things which belong to the Roman people and those things which owe a common use not to the Roman people merely, but to all men, and in the latter category he enumerates the sea.

Nor should it offend anyone that Celsus lays down a distinction between the shore and the sea, which are treated together by others. For, although with regard to the shore Celsus may have had his own idea (which that expression "I think" seems to indicate), nevertheless with regard to the sea he does not dissent from the others. And yet it seems to me more probable that the word "shore" is taken by Celsus not according to the Aquilian definition, insofar as waves run out therefrom,[46] but in a somewhat broader sense as is often wont to be done and as has been observed by the grammarians on that passage of Virgil: "The huge trunk lies on the shore."[47] This definition is proved from a passage of Paulus,[48] where, naming the shores nearest to the sea, he tacitly distinguishes them from the other shores which are farther distant from the sea and are therefore not an approach to the sea.[49] Meanwhile it can not be denied that the sea is expressly removed by Celsus from those things which belong to the Roman people. Neratius indeed says that even the shores (insofar as they are an approach to the sea) are not of the patrimony of the people, on the contrary he says that they belong to no one. His words are: "Whatever anyone has built on the shore will be his own, for the shores are not public in the same way as those things which are of the patrimony of the people, but as those things which were first produced by nature and have as yet come into the dominion of no one."[50] He could not have distinguished more clearly what belongs to no one from public property. But if Neratius

---

45. *Digest*, XLIII. 8. 3, pr., § 1.
46. *Institutes*, II. 1, § 3.
47. Virgil, *Aeneid*, II, 557.
48. *Digest*, XLI. 1. 65, § 1.
49. Compare Grotius, *De Jure Belli ac Pacis*, II. 3. 9.
50. *Digest*, XLI. 1. 14.

thought so with regard to the shore, with regard to the sea certainly he had no doubt, since, as we have said before, he attributed to the shore nothing in this regard except insofar as it is the last part of the sands of the sea and therefore a continuation of the sea.[51]

The third argument will be this, that the community of the sea is referred by the Roman jurists to a natural condition, which does not distinguish people from people. Pertinent hereto is that passage of Neratius just cited, ". . . as those things which were first produced by nature and have as yet come into the dominion of no one." Now it is certain that things when they were first created did not belong more to a people than to any man, and what even now has remained in its natural condition, occupied by no one, for instance, unknown and desolate islands, belongs to no people or prince. Hereto is also to be referred the statement of Marcianus and the Emperor Justinian, "*By the natural law* they are common to all,"[52] and of Ulpian, "The sea is *by nature* open to all."[53] For nations and kingdoms are not distinguished by nature but by human will. Therefore, in regard to those things which are common according to nature no people can have any preferential right over another people.

This reasoning is rightly explained by Faber when he says: "The sea and the shores have been left in their own right and primeval being, wherein all things were common; but rivers, ports, etc., are public, because they belong to the people so far as dominion goes."[54] Nothing could be said with greater truth or explicitness than this.[55] And so I wonder much at Welwod's statement that he has replied to this passage, for I certainly do not see what he has replied or even could reply. In point is that passage of Placentinus, praised likewise by Faber, that the sea itself is common and is under the dominion of no one save God,[56] the sense of which is as follows: Although many things under God as supreme Master receive other masters, nevertheless besides that supreme and first Master the sea has abso-

---

51. Compare Grotius, *De Jure Belli ac Pacis,* II. 3. 9.
52. *Digest,* I. 8. 2; *Institutes,* II. 1.
53. *Digest,* VIII. 4. 13.
54. Faber on *Institutes,* II. 1. 5.
55. Compare Grotius, *De Jure Belli ac Pacis,* II. 3. 10.
56. Placentinus on *Institutes,* II. 1. 1.

lutely no other master. Theophilus had said that "no master claimed it as his own property."[57] Otherwise if he had said nothing regarding the sea which was not applicable also to the land and other things, there would have been therein no "besides." Rightly therefore with David do we say that the land is the Lord God's,[58] but it will not be correct to say that it is under no other dominion save God's, unless to the word "dominion" is added the word "supreme," "absolute" or something similar.

Upon these arguments therefore our opinion rests, not only upon the word "common" which the jurists use. Consequently Welwod strikes at his own shadow, when he attacks this one argument rather seriously, and, to show that the word "common" is sometimes taken in a more restricted sense, cites the passage from Modestinus: "Rome is the common country,"[59] although nevertheless Modestinus would not write thus, but with a little more accuracy: "Rome is our common country." "Our," that is, as the constitution of Antoninus says, "of those who live in the Roman world."[60] But let Welwod show that in some place where it has been said "common to all men," where this word "common" is distinguished from the word "public," where it is added that it is common "by nature," that there it is to be understood as "common to the citizens of a single people," and then we shall confess that something has been brought forward by him which is not foreign to the subject.

The reason that the word "public" is sometimes applicable to the sea might seem more plausible, if this objection had not been met in the *Mare Liberum* with the surest of reasons. For since those things common to all (among which is the sea) are sometimes distinguished from those things which are public and sometimes are called public, it follows necessarily that the meaning of the word "public" is twofold. For sometimes the word is properly taken for that which belongs to the people and sometimes in a broader sense to include also those things which belong to the entire human race, by a metaphorical use of the word which is not obscure; because

57. Theophilus, *Paraphrasis Institutionum*, p. 219.
58. Psalms 24:1.
59. *Digest*, L. 1. 33.
60. *Digest*, I. 5. 17.

the human race is like a great people, and hence some philosophers call this world a city and themselves "cosmopolitans." Nor is this transferred use of the word "public" found only among the jurists. We have cited that noble passage of Ovid:

> . . . The use of water is *common:*
> *Nature* hath made nor sun nor air nor billowing waters
> Proper to one alone: I have come for gifts that are *public.*[61]

For Latona is speaking to the Lycians and she calls public what she had previously called common and indeed according to nature. Hence also come the following: "To publish a book," "To publish a corpus." It must likewise be noted that if "precision" (ἀκριβολογία) be sought, it should be referred particularly to those passages of the jurists where this controversy is treated *ex professo* and not where this argument is touched upon in passing. Now the more appropriate passage is that wherein is treated the division of property (*De rerum divisione*). There indeed the sea is not enumerated among the public things, but is separated from the public things as if "heterogeneous," as we have already shown. And what about the fact that the jurists themselves have given sufficient warning lest "the homonym" of the word "public" deceive anyone, as Neratius when he said that these "are not public in the same way as those things which are of the patrimony of the people, but as those things which were first produced by nature and have as yet come into the dominion of no one."[62] For manifestly there is here a distinction of an ambiguous word with regard to its signification, as if he were to say: "The word public indeed is properly taken for that which is of the people, as its origin indicates, but with regard to the sea and the shore it is taken in a special sense and means nothing else than common to all, belonging to no one." And so other jurists for the sake of distinction call these same things "public under the law of nations" to distinguish them from those things which are under the law of the people. For what the expression "under the law of nations" indicates is sufficiently shown by those passages of Marcianus and Justinian, where they say that villas

---

61. Ovid, *Metamorphoses,* VI, 349–51; cit. Grotius, *The Free Sea,* p. 25, above.
62. *Digest,* XLI. 1. 14.

and monuments must not be placed on the shore, "because they are not under the law of nations as is the sea,"[63] which Theophilus thus expresses: "For these things are not common to all men under the law of nations as is the sea."[64]

Let us conclude, therefore, from these very words of the Roman jurists that the sea is common to all and just as it was produced first by nature has come into the dominion of no one, and therefore is not in the patrimony of the people, is open by nature to all, is of the law of nations and its use common to all men.

From this let us proceed to infer that, if the use of the sea is common to all men, therefore no man should be prohibited from fishing on the sea. Thus the emperor says: "Because the use of the sea is public under the law of nations, therefore *everyone* is free to let down his nets from the sea,"[65] which Theophilus thus expresses: "It is granted to all who wish it to let down their nets from the sea."[66] Marcianus argues in a similar fashion: "By the natural law the sea and the shores of the sea are common *to all;* no one *therefore* is prohibited access to the shore of the sea for the sake of fishing."[67] In these passages should be noted the universal terms, "to all," "everyone," and "no one," and the universal cause, namely that the sea is "naturally common to all," for a universal cause produces a universal effect.

Similar is the following argument of Ulpian: "And yet a servitude upon the sea, which by nature is open to all, can not be imposed by private law,"[68] namely, that fishing be not exercised in a certain location. Here "emphasis" is not on the words "private law," but on the word "servitude"; but there has been added "by private law," because of the species of action which was in question, for that question had arisen between private individuals. The argument would have equal weight if you should say, "Servitude can not be imposed by people or prince upon that which is open

63. *Digest,* I. 8. 4; *Institutes,* II. 1, § 1.
64. Theophilus, *Paraphrasis Institutionum,* p. 210.
65. *Institutes,* II. 1, § 5.
66. Theophilus, *Paraphrasis Institutionum,* p. 212.
67. *Digest,* I. 8. 2.
68. *Digest,* VIII. 4. 13.

by nature to all," as if you were to say, "can not be imposed by a private individual"; for the force of the argument is evident in the particular words. The sea is open, that is, it is free, therefore it does not permit a servitude. It is open to all, therefore no one is to be excluded. It is open by nature to all, therefore there is no one who can make a decree against anyone else, since nature is no less potent against princes and peoples than against private individuals. Therefore he who prohibits anyone else from fishing on the sea, whoever he is, commits a wrong. Hence Ulpian: "If anyone is prohibited from fishing or navigating on the sea, use is to be made of action for damages,"[69] and in another passage: "Yet even this, that anyone may be prohibited from fishing before my house or camp, was made use of, although by no right; therefore, if anyone be prohibited, action for damages is still possible."[70]

Let there be a second conclusion therefore from the selfsame words of the jurists. Since the sea by its nature is open to all and its use is common to all men, it is licit for anyone to let down nets from the sea and no one is to be prohibited from access to the shore for the sake of fishing, and if anyone is prohibited from fishing on the sea, action for damages is possible.

And since this is so, and the very opinion included in the *Mare Liberum* is enunciated in almost the same words in the ancient authorities of Roman law, it is a marvel with what confidence Welwod dares to say that laws and responses (*responsa*) advanced in behalf of the freedom of the sea have nothing at all to do with the case. But no doubt an evil case borrows perfidy from boldness. Therefore, with these hushed but not crushed, he attempts to clothe his own pronouncements with unwonted antiquity by means of the testimony of the ancient jurists. But could he not have found anyone to say that the sea belonged to a prince or a single people, and its use was open to the citizens of only a single empire, and therefore foreigners could be prevented from fishing on the sea? None of these. For how could they say such things, after they had stated so roundly that the sea was not in the patrimony of a people, but was open by nature to all, and

69. *Digest*, XLIII. 8. 2, § 9.
70. *Digest*, XLVII. 10. 13, § 7.

that its use was common to all men, and that no one should be prohibited from fishing? For the jurists were not so simple as to dissent so openly from themselves, nor Tribonianus and his helpers so stupid as to insert in a single *Corpus,* as being entirely consistent, statements which were manifestly contradictory. Not therefore ingenuity, but material was lacking here to Welwod for erecting this edifice.

Nevertheless let us see what he could finally adduce. "The words of Ulpian," he says, "I read to the following effect: *There are some who think* action for damages is possible to me."[71] But you who have read these words, have you not read also those presented a little below, where Ulpian makes the clear assertion: "If anyone is prohibited, action for damages is possible," and indeed in a more serious question.[72] For in the earlier words "in his thesis" the question is raised whether action for damages is competent to him who is prohibited from fishing on the sea or letting down his nets; but in the later words "in the hypothesis" which is of more difficult controversy, whether action for damages is competent also to him who is prohibited from fishing before the villa or camp of another, when it is taken for granted that he could be prohibited. Nevertheless Ulpian replies definitely καὶ διαρρήδην (and explicitly) that action is possible.

It is customary for the jurists as well as the philosophers to speak at first after the manner of one doubting so that, when the question has been aired from every side, they might finally ornament and adorn the truth. So it is a fixed rule that in responses attention should be paid to the last part, because this contains the jurist's own opinion. Had Welwod done this, he would not have struck that statement "There are some who think," especially if he had been willing to consult still another passage of Ulpian, where without any hesitation he declares: "If anyone be prohibited from fishing or navigating on the sea, use is to be made of action for damages."[73]

Yet in order that it be more correctly understood what Ulpian intended by those words "There are some who think," it must be noted that the doubt does not consist in whether he who prohibits another from fishing

71. *Digest,* XLVII. 10. 13, § 7.
72. *Digest,* XLVII. 10. 13, § 7.
73. *Digest,* XLIII. 8. 2, § 9.

has committed an injustice, that is, "a wrong" (ἀδίκημα), but whether he is bound by action for damages. For these are quite different things, and it is very clear from other examples adduced in the same response. "If anyone in decreeing honors, does not allow, for instance, an image or something else of this character to be decreed to some one, is he bound by action for damages; and Labeo says he is not bound, although he may have done it for the sake of disgrace."[74] He then goes on to say: "If duties or burdens are imposed on someone by way of damage, if sentence is imposed by way of damage, action for damages is not possible."[75] But there is in all these "a wrong" (ἀδίκημα); nor is this questioned, but whether action for damages should be granted. So also he who prohibits another from fishing undoubtedly "does wrong" (ἀδικεῖ), for, as Ulpian says in that very passage: "The sea is common to all just as also the air," but whether action for damages is competent against him is open to doubt.

The reason for doubt seems to have been this, that some have thought action for damages, just as other actions also, pertain only to what is done contrary to civil law and not to what is done contrary to the law of nations. So Pomponius says that he who builds on the sea has no civil action *De faciendo*.[76] Therefore some, it seems, have thought that he who impedes fishing should be prohibited rather by force, just as in the same passage Pomponius said that he who with great disadvantage to others builds on the sea or on the shore should be prohibited by force. Not dissimilar is the fact that the interdict *Uti possidetis* is not granted to him who is prohibited from fishing on the sea by the common law, and the reason for this Papinian adduces: because interdicts are applicable to private cases, not to public ones.[77] Also the fact that Ulpian says that the interdict *Ne quid in loco publico fiat*[78] is not competent to him who is prohibited from fishing or navigating on the sea, while Labeo replied that, if anything is done on the sea whereby the way for navigation is made worse, since the proper inter-

74. *Digest,* XLVII. 10. 13, § 4.
75. *Digest,* XLVII. 10. 13, § 5.
76. *Digest,* XLI. 1. 50.
77. *Digest,* XLVII. 10. 14.
78. *Digest,* XLIII. 8. 2, § 9.

dict *Ne quid in flumine* could not be granted, a useful interdict conceived after the following manner, *Ne quid in mari*, is competent.[79]

In all of these passages there is no question about the injustice of an action by which the use of a common thing is impeded, but about the proper remedy. Now although this doubt had some color, because the formulae of actions were found in the civil law, not in the law of nations, nevertheless concession has deservedly been made to the opinion that action for damages should be granted, because it has been established not only by the law of nations, but also by the civil law of the Romans, namely in rescripts of the emperors, that no one should be prohibited from fishing.

This is the reason why Ulpian added to his response: "And it has been very often handed down in rescripts that no one can be prohibited from fishing,"[80] namely because the constitutions of the emperors form a very powerful part of the civil law.[81] The law of nations sufficed to make the prohibition illicit, but that under this name a civil action be competent, the authority of the civil law from which civil actions emanate, was or certainly could seem to be necessary. But as to Welwod's inference from this and from a not dissimilar passage of Marcianus, that those opinions of prudent men rest on the authority of the emperor,[82] if he means that this which makes for his proposition rests primarily on that authority and that law derives its origin from the will of the emperors, manifestly this is opposed not only to those other responses which we have mentioned above, but also to those very passages of Ulpian and Marcianus.

"The sea," says Ulpian, "is common to all and the shores, just as the air, and it has been very often handed down in rescripts that no one can be prohibited from fishing."[83] In the first place he posits the law of nations when he says that the sea is common just as the air, then by the interposition of the copulative conjunction he shows that this itself is approved

---

79. *Digest,* XLIII. 12. 1, § 17.
80. *Digest,* XLVII. 10. 13, § 7.
81. *Institutes,* I. 2, § 3.
82. Welwod, "Of the Community and Propriety of the Seas," p. 68, above.
83. *Digest,* XLVII. 10. 13, § 17.

also by the civil law. So also Marcianus: "By the natural law the following are common to all: air, running water and the sea and therefore the shores of the sea; no one therefore is prohibited access to the shore of the sea, provided however he abstains from villas and buildings and monuments, because they are not of the law of nations as is the sea; and this is what the Emperor Pius wrote in a rescript to the Formian and Capenatan fishermen."[84] I shall not dispute whether the Emperor Pius wrote in his rescript that no one should be prohibited from fishing, or whether he should refrain from villas and buildings, which is probable, because there is a similar rescript of the same emperor to birdcatchers: "It is not in keeping with the wishes of the emperor that you should hunt on others' lands."[85] But, as I say, I shall not unwillingly grant that the Emperor Pius wrote in a rescript that no one should be prohibited from fishing. Didn't Marcianus clearly, before the rescript of Emperor Pius, posit a natural law? Then he said: "and this the Emperor Pius also wrote in a rescript," that is, besides the fact that this has been established by the law of nature or of nations, we have also a rescript of the Emperor Pius in harmony with the natural law. Who will infer from this that that law sprang from the will of the emperor and will not see that the contrary rather is contained in those words?

It is quite well-known that by the rescripts of a prince not always is a new law established or an ambiguity cleared up, but often new guards and sanctions are added to an old and well-known law. By the divine law it was clearly enough established what should be thought and taught about the Highest Trinity, yet the same is prescribed in the constitutions of the emperors.[86] That children should be loved by parents and parents by children is commanded by the law of nature,[87] yet the same thing was done by a Senatusconsultum.[88] The freedom of a blameless defense proceeds from the law of nature, yet that this is licit has been handed down in rescripts by the emperors.[89] The law of nations demands that contracts be fulfilled,

---

84. *Digest*, I. 8. 2, § 1; *Digest*, I. 8. 4.
85. *Digest*, VIII. 3. 16.
86. *Code*, I. 1.
87. *Institutes*, I. 2.
88. *Senatusconsultum Plancianum;* cf. *Digest*, XXV. 3. 1, §§ 14, 15.
89. *Code*, VIII. 4. 1.

nevertheless there are many statutes on this subject. And rightly all this, for the Prince is not only the legislator of the civil law, but the guardian and vindicator of the divine law, the natural law, and the law of nations. Falsely therefore does Welwod, from the fact that emperors have issued rescripts concerning the nonprohibition of fishing, infer that they have claimed for themselves ownership over the sea.[90] Such argumentation would not proceed even in those cases wherein some new law has been established by the emperors, for princes make laws also with regard to the property of others, and the "law-making" ($\nu o\mu o\theta\epsilon\tau\iota\kappa\grave{\eta}$) power comes from sovereignty, not from ownership. Hence the statement of Seneca: "Everything is under the sovereignty of Caesar, his own things in his patrimony."[91]

Welwod proceeds to ask to whom did the emperors issue such rescripts, was it not to their subjects? Therefore the use of the seas should be common only to the subjects.[92] Again a wonderful deduction, as if it were said: "The king wrote to his subjects not to despoil anyone except a public enemy; therefore immunity from depredation is due to subjects alone." Who does not see that there is considerable difference between the one for whom the law is laid down and the one whom the law benefits? A precept is given to fishermen subjects; but it is prescribed that they prohibit no one from fishing, without any distinction whether he be a subject or not. And yet even if the emperors had clearly forbidden their subjects to be prohibited from fishing, not even in this way could it be inferred that therefore foreigners could be prohibited. For what is affirmed of one species is not forthwith denied of another. Indeed on the contrary what is affirmed of a genus is rightly affirmed of the individual species. Consequently, not because it is proper to this species is it therefore improper to another. Moreover, that that statement "that no one be prohibited from fishing" is competent to a first genus and not to a species, that is, to subjects, is shown by those opinions which say that the use of the sea is common to all men and the sea is by nature open to all. For the phrase "to all men" denotes a ge-

90. Welwod, "Of the Community and Propriety of the Seas," p. 68, above.
91. Seneca, *De beneficiis*, VII. 6. 3.
92. Welwod, "Of the Community and Propriety of the Seas," p. 68, above.

nus, not a species, and what is natural can not be proper to that species which is distinguished from another not by nature but by institution.

There follows another argument of Welwod taken from Pomponius, wherein he said: "Although what is erected on the shore becomes ours, yet the decree of the praetor should be applied in order that it be licit to do this."[93] I shall not say that the question of building is different from the question of fishing; that by building that becomes one's own which owed a common use, while by fishing only that which formerly simply belonged to no one. The very name of praetor shows well enough that no proper right to the sea or the shore either of people or of prince was indicated in that passage. For the Roman praetor had no administration of the property of the people while the commonwealth was free, nor of the property of the prince after the commonwealth was changed. Therefore he could not have granted anything out of the property of the people to anyone, but such a concession would have to be made either by a law, that is, by the will of the Roman people, or by a Senatusconsultum or by an edict or decree of the emperors, as is clearly witnessed in the formula of the interdict *Ne quid in loco publico*.[94] Now the praetor, as the same M. Pomponius teaches elsewhere, was established for this purpose, to render the law;[95] and that his functions have not been otherwise is very evident from all Roman history. Hence the statement of Cicero: "Let the praetor be the advocate of the law who shall judge or order to be judged private affairs."[96]

Falsely, therefore, does Welwod, in that passage wherein the decree of the praetor is treated, interpose another passage of Ulpian which pertains to the concession of an emperor. For Ulpian treats not of the shore or of the sea, but of the property of the people or even of a municipality. For when he was interpreting the edict *Quod vi aut clam* and had said that an exception should be granted to him who had done something with the permission of the possessor, he added that this permission should be so accepted not only if he whose property it was had permitted it, but also if

93. *Digest,* XLI. 1. 50.
94. *Digest,* XLIII. 8. 2.
95. *Digest,* I. 2. 2, § 27.
96. Cicero, *De legibus,* III. 3. 8.

the overseer, guardian or manager [had permitted it], because all these have the right of making the concession.[97] But if the head or manager of the commonwealth had permitted [some one] to do something in a public matter, he says that an exception was written by Nerva: unless it were not permitted to take place, because indeed he had permitted who had not the right of permitting. For although, he says, the superintendence of public places is given to the head and manager of the commonwealth, nevertheless the concession was not given.

We see here that no mention has been made of the praetor, as one who has neither the superintendence nor concession. Afterwards Ulpian says that this reply of Nerva is true, if municipal law makes no further concession, that is, the power (*arbitrium*) of conceding, to the manager of the commonwealth. But that, if by the prince or by him to whom the prince shall have granted this right (*jus*) of conceding (in the affairs namely of the Roman people), the same should be approved: namely that in that case an exception was to be admitted. Who therefore does not see "to a human head a horse's neck joined."[98] For Pomponius treats of the shore, Ulpian of the soil proper to a people or municipality; Pomponius of a decree of the praetor, that is, a judge, Ulpian of the concession of an owner or of him who acts in place of an owner; the owner or he who acts in his place gives the right to one who does not have it, the praetor declares what the right is and corroborates it by his authority.

But that it may be more correctly understood in what direction this decree of the praetor looks, it must be noted that what we have built on the shore becomes ours by the law of nations even without a decree of the praetor. "If anyone builds on the sea or on the shore," says Ulpian, "he makes it his own by the law of nations."[99] And Justinian says that since the use of the shores is public "by the law of nations," therefore anyone at all is free to place his house there.[100] And Scaevola: "It is licit *by the law of nations* to build on the shore."[101] And Neratius says that that which any-

97. *Digest,* XLIII. 24. 3, §§ 2–4.
98. Horace, *Ars poetica,* 1.
99. *Digest,* XXXIX. 1. 1, § 18.
100. *Institutes,* II. 1, § 5.
101. *Digest,* XLIII. 8. 4.

one has built on the shore is his own, because the shores are in the same category as those things which were first produced by nature.[102] Hence it is surely evident that both the right of building and ownership of the soil which has been built upon come from the law of nations as from a sole and sufficient cause. But by the law of nations this rule has the following exception: "unless public use is impeded," as Scaevola says,[103] "unless he does this to the inconvenience of the rest," as Pomponius says,[104] "unless the thing will be harmful to others," as Ulpian said,[105] "unless the use of the sea or of the shore become impaired," which are the words of Celsus.[106] Therefore if anyone builds to the hindrance of public use, he, as Pomponius says, may be forcibly prevented.[107]

Hence will arise the great evil of conflicts and fights, if this one says he is building without hindrance to public use, while that one asserts public use is impeded. "Now why," said Julian of old, "should the praetor allow those to proceed to arms and conflict whom he can compose by his own jurisdiction?"[108] And that this was the meaning of Pomponius is evident from a similar statement of Paulus. "That is not to be conceded to individuals," he says, "which may be done publicly through a magistrate, lest there be occasion for greater tumult."[109] Now it must be noted that this opinion of Paulus was taken from Book XIII to Plautius, in which he makes another fragment, cited from the same book, amply prove that he was dealing with the sea and the shore.[110] And I scarcely doubt but that Paulus wrote this upon the same passage of Plautius from which Pomponius drew his statement about using a decree. For that that statement of Pomponius also was from Plautius, the inscription shows.

Not therefore because *per se* no one has sufficient right to build on the shore without hindrance to common use is a decree required; but lest there

---

102. *Digest*, XLI. 1. 14.
103. *Digest*, XLIII. 8. 4.
104. *Digest*, XLI. 1. 50.
105. *Digest*, XLIII. 8. 2, § 8.
106. *Digest*, XLIII. 8. 3, § 1.
107. *Digest*, XLI. 1. 50.
108. *Digest*, VII. 1. 13, § 3.
109. *Digest*, L. 17. 176.
110. *Digest*, XLVII. 10. 14.

be occasion for greater tumult, if one denies and another asserts that the common use is impeded. Consequently it is better to have in advance the cognizance of the praetor as to whether the common use is impeded or not. Therefore those words "the praetor's decree must be used, that it may be licit to do it" must be accepted with regard to the permissibility of fact, not of right. It is licit before the decree by the law of nations, but it is not safe. For it will be easy to find one who will wish to prevent forcibly; and if this is done, what formula will he try, since no interdict and not even a civil action has been put forth against such a deed? But if the praetor has interposed his cognizance, the one prohibited will be fortified not only by the law of nations, but by civil law also, and he will have someone to whom he may have recourse.

And this is what Ulpian said: "If no one is perceptibly injured, he who builds on the shore must be protected,"[111] he must be protected namely by the office and authority of the praetor. So elsewhere the same Ulpian says that in order that anyone may demolish forcibly what another has built forcibly, he should proceed in no other way than from a great and necessary cause; otherwise all these things should be carried out by the office of the judge.[112] Rightly therefore did Accursius say, in explanation of the response of Pomponius, that if the building did no injury to anyone, it would be valid even without a decree.[113] For Pomponius had not said that a decree must be used for that which is built to become ours, nevertheless a decree must be used. In brief, where there is doubt whether public use is impeded by the building or not, a decree should be used, not because right is wanting, but because it is to the interest of the peace of subjects that it be done so; nor is the right granted by the decree, but the right is declared to be what it is and is placed beyond controversy.

Since therefore we have proved by the testimony of so many notable authorities that the use of the sea is common to all men by the law of nations and that consequently no one can be prevented from fishing, and since no patron of the opposite opinion can be adduced from all antiquity,

---

111. *Digest,* XLIII. 8. 2, § 8.
112. *Digest,* XLIII. 24. 7, § 3.
113. Accursius on *Digest,* XLI. 1. 50.

I think the case is complete, even if I shall have adduced no reason why it should be so. For I do not see what is to prevent the dictum, that a reason can not be given for everything which has been established, from being extended also to certain precepts of the law of nations, especially if the reason be such that therefrom the precepts emanate as a necessary consequence.

For example, in the marriage of persons who are joined by proximate ties of blood or affinity, even if we did not have the written law of God, nevertheless it would by no means be licit to ignore that such a union is illicit, since the Roman jurists say that any such is incest by the law of nations[114] and the Apostle Paul says that such a crime "was not even mentioned among the gentiles."[115] Now if anyone wishes to give a reason for this precept, he will not easily find one to which no objection can be made, or equally certain and evident as is the precept itself. And surely what need to scrutinize causes, when these are to be referred "to the judgment of God."[116] For in these also "the nations disclose the work of the law written in their hearts, their conscience bearing witness to them."[117]

Rightly therefore in the *Institutes* are the natural laws, among which are also to be included certain precepts of the law of nations, said to have been established by a certain divine providence.[118] Hence not dissimilar is that phrase of Sophocles, "the unwritten and immutable laws of the Gods,"[119] concerning which he also adds the following: "and no one knows whence they sprang."[120] Not otherwise is Isocrates: "An ancient custom under which all men continue to live, not as resting upon the nature of man, but as having been prescribed by the power of the deity."[121] Therefore this very fact, that God has insinuated such precepts in the minds of men, is sufficient to induce obligation even if no reason is apparent.

---

114. *Digest,* XXIII. 2. 68.
115. I Corinthians 5:1.
116. Romans 1:32.
117. Romans 2:15.
118. *Institutes,* I. 2, § 11.
119. Sophocles, *Antigone,* 454.
120. Ibid., 457.
121. Isocrates, *Panathenaic,* 268.

Again, there are other precepts of the law of nations which have their origin in tacit consent. These likewise can induce obligation even if none of them is a certain consequence of natural principles. Of this kind seems to be the precept with regard to the admittance of ambassadors. For just as among a single people, even if that people is not adapted to legislation, nevertheless usage and custom itself, which is the index of tacit consent, makes law, so also the primitive custom of the human race has the force of law. And hence it is that much of the law of nations is said to have been introduced by customs. Pertinent hereto is the statement in the *Institutes,* that the human nations established certain laws for themselves.[122] Now these precepts, whether they arise from divine instinct or consent of the nations, are testified to both by the most ancient usage of civilized nations and by the authority of the wisest men. Since they abundantly support us in every particular in defense of the community of the sea, deservedly would this likewise have force as a precept of the law of nations even if the reason were obscure why it should have been thus established.

And here by the way we should correct the error of Welwod when he teaches that, whenever in this argument of the sea mention is made of the law of nations, it is not to be understood that a law made by the common consent of the nations, but only an example of the custom of other nations, is brought to our attention, as if the jurists intended to say: "The freedom of fishing in our seas and of doing a certain work on our shores is competent to every subject of the Roman Empire, just as the same fishing and right of doing work is competent to the subjects of other nations on their own seas and shores." I do not wish to deny that sometimes, in the historians especially, the law of nations is taken improperly, not for that law which the nations have between themselves, but for that which certain nations, one following the example of another, have determined upon as law for themselves, that is, for the civil law of the different peoples. But this meaning, apart from being improper and rather rare, can not at all have place here. For we have shown above from the opinion of the jurists that the sea owes a common use to all men; but things which are of such

---

122. *Institutes,* I. 2, § 11.

a character are not governed by a civil law of one or more peoples but by the common law of nations. For the civil law governs those matters which pertain to the association of a single people, while the law of nations regulates those which look to the common association of the human race.

Now add the fact that the sea is not only said by the jurists to be common by the law of nations, but without any addition it is said to be of the right (*jus*) of nations. In these passages "right" (*jus*) can not mean a norm of justice, but a moral faculty over a thing, as when we say "this thing is of my right (*jus*), that is, I have ownership over it or use or something similar." Besides, the same jurists, when they deal in this argument with law (*jus*) as the norm of justice, not only say that the sea is common by the law of nations, but in place of the same law of nations they frequently use the term natural law, as is clear from the *Institutes*. But this word can not be stretched to that law of nations improperly so-called, that is, to the law common by imitation to certain peoples. For nature is a universal principle, and those things which are natural are extended to all of the same nature, not by chance but by primitive destination. And therefore Aristotle defines "natural law" as "that which has the same force everywhere," and so he distinguishes from that law "that which from the beginning did not differ in this or another way."[123]

We think nevertheless that the reason adduced by us why the sea can not become the property of any one is such that no one can prove it vain. Now it is such, because ownership of property began with natural possession, as Nerva the Younger says,[124] and it can be shown "inductively." But the sea can not be possessed naturally, neither its entirety nor any part which may remain joined and united to its entirety. For natural possession is, according to the definition of Theophilus, "a holding fast of a physical thing."[125] Paulus expressed the Greek κατέχειν (to hold fast) in Latin by "tenere" (to hold), and with Nerva makes its beginning to be apprehension.[126] Now nothing can be apprehended unless limited corporally. But it

---

123. Aristotle, *Nicomachean Ethics*, V. 7. 1 (1134b 23).
124. *Digest*, XLI. 2. 1, § 1.
125. Theophilus, *Paraphrasis Institutionum*, p. 889.
126. *Digest*, XLI. 2. 1; *Digest*, XLI. 2. 1, § 1.

is the nature of liquids to be limited by something else; and accordingly liquids can not be possessed except by means of that whereby they are limited, as wine is possessed by means of a vessel, rivers by means of their banks. Therefore an unlimited liquid is not to be possessed. But of such a character is the sea, and the river after it has passed outside of its banks; so far from it being possible for them to be possessed, on the contrary whatever is held by them ceases to be possessed.

Hence Labeo, Nerva, Paulus say that I cease to possess that place which the river or sea has occupied.[127] And hence it is that, just as what has been built on the sea becomes private property (that is of the builder, because the sand under the sea has been limited by the building and is apprehended), so what has been occupied on the sea becomes public, as Aristo said[128]—a statement which Neratius explains when he says that after the building which had been erected on the shore has been removed (for in this matter there is the same principle with regard to the shore as with regard to any maritime sea), the place does not remain his whose building it was, but reverts to its pristine condition and therefore becomes public as if there had been no building there.[129] But he had said a little previously that by "public" in this matter should be understood not that which is a people's but that which belongs to no one. Marcianus explaining the same thing says that the place, after the building is destroyed, reverts as if by the right of postliminium.[130] Why, unless because only that part of the sea or shore can be possessed which is apprehended corporally, and the rest can not be possessed. Therefore the real reason why the sea can not become the property of anyone is expressed by Jean Faber, *On the Institutes:* "Because the sea is unapprehendable as is the air, therefore it was not connected with the property of the people."[131]

Now let us see how Welwod has attacked this reasoning. First, he says,

127. *Digest,* XLI. 2. 3, § 17; *Digest,* XLI. 2. 30, § 3.
128. *Digest,* I. 8. 10.
129. *Digest,* XLVI. 1. 14, § 1.
130. *Digest,* I. 8. 6.
131. Faber on *Institutes,* II. 1, § 5.

the lack of solidity and the fact that it can not be trod upon in any manner, these do "not hinder the solid possession of it, far less the occupation and acquiring, if we will give to the sea, that which the jurisconsults indulgently grant to the land."[132] Then he cites the response of Paulus which is in full as follows: "It is not to be accepted in the sense that he who wishes to possess an estate walks around all the land (*glebas*), but it is sufficient for him to enter any part of his estate, provided he has this intention and thought, namely that he wishes to possess the estate to its limit."[133] Who does not see that this argumentation is vicious in a number of ways? To prove that a thing which is not solid and which can not be trod upon can be possessed, an example is adduced from an estate, that is, from a thing which is solid and can be trod upon. Then it is said that that must be granted to the sea which is granted to the land. But what is that? Namely that it is sufficient to have entered and walked upon a part? But there is no part of the sea which can be walked upon.

It is added that, if possession could not be impeded, much less could occupation be impeded. But the situation is far different; for since occupation is the cause of possession, more is accordingly required for it. For example, in the case of a wild beast, it should be captured and apprehended to be first occupied, while afterwards it is sufficient if it be guarded in any manner whatsoever. "For they are possessed," as Nerva the Younger says, "insofar as they are under our custody."[134] He learnedly explains this as follows: "Since, if we wish, we can gain natural possession," where natural possession is apprehension itself. Therefore for occupation the act of apprehension is required, for possession the power of apprehension is sufficient. And this indeed in the case of movables. But in the case of immovables, intention is sufficient for the retention of possession which has been begun by intention and physical apprehension.[135] Therefore possession occurs much more easily than occupation and first acquisition.

132. Welwod, "Of the Community and Propriety of the Seas," p. 70, above.
133. *Digest*, XLI. 2. 3, § 1.
134. *Digest*, XLI. 2. 3, § 13.
135. *Digest*, XLI. 2. 3, § 7; *Digest*, XLI. 2. 25.

But to press the point, the jurists describe possession in the case of movables by the physical apprehension (*manuum prehensione*),[136] while in the case of immovables by the power of standing and sitting. Therefore that which can not be apprehended and can not be stood or sat upon, can not *per se* be possessed. Yet *per aliud* such a thing can be possessed, if it is comprehended in a more solid substance by which it may be possessed; for the contents are possessed by means of the container. The sea can not *per se* be apprehended, stood or sat upon. For it to be possessed *per aliud*, it would be necessary to establish two things, that the sea is contained by something else and that this container is possessed by someone—which it is quite certain does not happen.

With regard to the response of Paulus, there is no question there of the first occupation of the estate; for that estate under discussion had already been limited, as is clear from the words of the jurist. Now to limit a thing which belongs to no one is to occupy it, and without limitation occupation does not proceed. But once a thing has been occupied and limited, possession afterwards proceeds more easily, not indeed without physical apprehension, but in such a way that the act of the body over one part may be extended to the whole which has previously been limited physically. This too not otherwise unless there be something to hinder it. So if an army attacks with great violence an estate previously possessed by another, it obtains only that part which it has entered.[137] Therefore there are three reasons why the response of Paulus can not be applied to the sea; because the sea has not been physically limited or fenced off by anyone, because not even any part of it can be stood upon, because the sea is opposed to possession in such a way that an extension can not be made from a part to the whole. For that the sea is opposed to possession is clear from the fact that even the sands of the sea, once occupied by some building or pier in such a way that they have become someone's property, cease to be the property of the occupier after the building or pier has been destroyed.[138] Whence it also follows: even if any navigator could be said to have ob-

---

136. *Digest*, XLI. 2. 1; *Digest*, XLI. 2. 3, § 5.
137. *Digest*, XLI. 2. 18, § 4.
138. Compare *Digest*, XLI. 1. 14, § 1.

tained possession of the sea or any part of it (which is by no means so, because he who navigates does not stand on the sea, does not hold the sea, "does not hold fast," but rather "is even held fast"),[139] yet after the departure of the ship possession likewise would straightway cease.

Therefore the proximate reason why the sea can not be possessed is neither its fluid nature nor its "continually flowing to and fro" (which Welwod brings up against himself in vain),[140] but its incomprehensibility the same as in the case of the air. Meanwhile that vigorous motion of the sea, as the untamed instinct in wild beasts, would make it impossible, even if occupation took place here, for possession to be continued, and ownership through possession, unless by a perpetual and close guardianship.

Welwod proceeds to say that, although the sea is fluid in its parts, nevertheless by reason of its entirety it retains its own limits which it scarcely transgresses. If Welwod concedes that for the initiating of possession it is required that the thing be limited, while the parts of the sea cohering in the whole are not acknowledged to be terminated, it must be acknowledged at the same time that at least the parts of the sea could not be occupied. Again, if he concedes, which is true, that a thing which is fluid and (to use the word) not stand-on-able, is not possessed otherwise than through the possession of a terminator which is stand-on-able, while he wishes this terminator to be the maritime shore, it will follow that the whole sea is not possessed, because no one possesses all the maritime shores at the same time. Add now the fact that not even the maritime shores are the limits of the sea; for the lands are girdled by the sea, the sea goes around "and surrounds" the lands, as all the Latin and Greek geographers and authorities call it. And reason makes it clear; for parts of the earth do not cohere, all the sea properly so-called coheres and is one and continuous. Therefore great parts of land are islands of the sea and are so-called by noteworthy writers, while islands are *in salo* (in the brine) whence their name. Therefore the limit of lands is the air and sea, the limit of the entire sea is only the air.

Then Welwod acknowledges that "not in every part of the sea" are there

---

139. cf. Grotius, *The Free Sea*, p. 32, above.
140. Welwod, "Of the Community and Propriety of the Seas," p. 70, above.

islands, shallows, rocks, by which marks are distinguished "the limits of the divisible parts."[141] But when he says this, he takes too much for granted. For no one has said that any part of the sea which is united to its entirety can be physically divided; but an intellectual division posits nothing in fact and does not make for possession. So islands, shallows, rocks standing out in the sea do not physically limit the sea, but are limited by the sea; nevertheless they can be of service in directing intellectual lines and so placing intellectual limits. But this too does not make for possession.

Welwod urges: "But God," he says, ". . . hath given an understanding heart to man," which is capable of such a distinction by means of assisting instruments, such as the nautical compass, the astrolabium, etc. I admit that the sea can be distinguished and that there is a certain use for this distinction, both in matters which the intellect performs *per se,* such as geographical observations, and in matters which the intellect performs with the aid of the will, to which contracts of men should be referred. And consequently if any treaties had been made which rested on such a distinction, I said in the *Mare Liberum* that the thing is not affected but the persons are obligated.[142] But for the purpose of seeking ownership those considerations are not pertinent. For ownership does not occur without possession, while possession does not begin with the intention only, but an act of the body must be added.[143] But if the drawing of an intellectual line were sufficient for this matter, what the laws dictate would already be false, namely that we do not obtain possession by intention. Moreover, it is a wonder that Welwod does not solve that surest of arguments, which he himself calls "a scoff," namely, if the drawing of a line were sufficient for occupation, the astronomers should be said to be the possessors of the heaven and the geometers of the earth.

Although that rule of law is well known, namely that possession does not begin by an act of the mind, nevertheless if anyone stubbornly op-

141. Welwod, "Of the Community and Propriety of the Seas," p. 71, above.
142. Grotius, *The Free Sea,* p. 31, above; compare Grotius, *De Jure Belli ac Pacis,* II. 3. 15.
143. *Digest,* XLI. 2. 3, § 1.

posed it, its proof is at hand in the manifest absurdity of the contrary. For if possession were begun by an act of the mind, and with possession ownership, since two at the same time could exercise the same act of the mind with regard to the same thing, it would follow that both obtain possession of the thing and ownership over the whole. This is as impossible in law, as the jurist Paulus says, as it is impossible in nature for two bodies to be in the same place at the same time.[144] Besides, acts of the mind are not visible, and therefore it can not be known which of the two exercised an act of the mind first, and accordingly the ownership of property would be uncertain. But all this is different in the physical act of occupation, for two can not exercise that on the same body at the same time. For, as Paulus says, it is against nature that you seem to hold what I hold.[145] Then too, such an act is visible and consequently capable of proof, so that it can be known which of two first occupied the property, and therefore who is the certain owner of the property,

With a few words interjected, with which we shall soon deal, he cites this statement of Papinian: "In questions of boundaries old monuments are to be followed."[146] But what is this to the point? For the judgment of regulating boundaries, as Ulpian said, refers to rural lands.[147] None of the ancients teaches us that the sea comes under this judgment. Then from a thesis to an hypothesis he drags me against my will. I humbly respect the majesty of the King of Britain and do not think any empire could fall to his lot commensurate with his excellent virtues. But although he deserves much greater things, it is to be set down among his praises that he is content with its present size and surpasses the great deeds of his forbears by coveting nothing. Then too, so great is his sense of justice towards all, and singular his benevolent attitude toward allies and associates, that the Batavians dare to hope from his goodness many things which are not due them by right. But because he has interjected something about the English

144. *Digest,* XLI. 2. 3, § 5.
145. *Digest,* XLI. 2. 3, § 5.
146. *Digest,* X. 1. 11.
147. *Digest,* X. 1. 2.

islands, and even the "covenant twixt Scottish men and Hollanders," I shall set forth these truths again.

A very learned man, Professor at the University of Cambridge, who has reduced English law to the method of the Justinian *Institutes,* under the title "On the division of property" distinguishes things which are common by natural law from things which are public.[148] Among the things common by natural law he places the sea, and the shores of the sea as if accessory. Consequently, he says, no one is prohibited access to the shore of the sea, provided however he abstains from villas and buildings, because, he says, the shores are common by the law of nations just as the sea also. Then passing over to the second group, he says rivers and ports are public. But these public things, he says, which were at one time the entire people's, are transferred by our law to the King, namely, him who sustains the person of all the people and consequently of the commonwealth itself. Therefore those who today build ships on the banks of public rivers under this name pay a tax to the King or those who exercise his right; and in a public river no one fishes who has not obtained this license from the King.

Now in the treaty, which was entered into in 1495 between Henry VII, king of England, and Philip, ruler of Holland and Zeeland,[149] there are the following words "With regard to the fishermen of either party of the aforenamed parties, of whatsoever condition they may be, they shall be able everywhere to go, sail over the sea, fish in security without any hindrance, license or safe-conduct." And with regard to this treaty, so far as it pertains to fishing, nothing new has been added in later acts. Again in that treaty, which was agreed to in 1540 between James VI,[150] king of Scotland, and Maria, queen of Hungary, as ruler of Belgium and specifically of Holland and Zeeland, there was provision with regard to the immunity of fishermen.[151] But in another of the year 1550, the Emperor Charles, ruler of Holland and Zeeland, and the same King James of Scotland promise

---

148. John Cowell (regius professor of civil law, University of Cambridge), *Institutiones juris Anglicani ad methodam Institutionem imperialium compositae et digestae,* pp. 48–64 ("De rerum divisione et adquirendo earum dominio").

149. The "Intercursus Magnus" (1496).

150. sc. James V of Scotland.

151. Treaty of Binche (1541).

that those agreements concerning fishing and the free use of the sea would be observed sincerely.[152] The words of this treaty were repeated in the latest treaty which in the year 1594 the greatest of rulers, James, then king of Scotland, now of all Britain and Ireland, made with the United Estates of our nations.[153] To these treaties and the law of nations with which those treaties are in harmony, the usage likewise and custom of time antedating all memory of man are added. For in every age the Batavian fishermen have fished freely under the very shores of England and Scotland no less than in the other parts of the ocean, nor have they allowed themselves to be hindered in any way in that use of liberty; so that even if prescription should have any place here, so far from possibly being put forward against them, it would manifestly be in their favor.

Now as to the fact that Welwod labors to show that succession of parts does not hinder possession, and points to Alfenus[154] for testimony to prove that with the gradual changing of the particles the thing does not become something else, he tires himself needlessly. For nonoccupability does not properly rest upon this foundation nor does the comparison proceed correctly. For the parts of a region, a ship or a man are not changed by a certain impetus simultaneously, but little by little and entirely insensibly, while the parts of the sea stand still at no moment. But as to his repetition here that the entire body of the sea is restrained as it were in its own limits, this is not pertinent to the subject. For if he means that the essence of the sea is finite, it does not follow hence that it is occupable; for the element of the air also is finite. If he means besides that the sea is limited by the land, it has already been shown above that the land is not the entire limit of the entire sea. Indeed the land is not the entire limit of parts of the sea, which in the mind constitute a certain entirety *per se,* such as the Spanish, French, Cimbrian Sea, for no such sea is surrounded by land.

Up to this point indeed we have forged the physical reason why the sea could not become property. We add another moral reason why it seems the sea should not become property. Let us remember what Aristotle said,

152. Treaty of Binche (1550).
153. Treaty of Edinburgh (1594).
154. *Digest,* V. 1. 76.

that in a moral matter "proofs" (ἀποδείξεις) are not given, but we ought here "seek out the precision which the nature of the thing admits of."[155] We have shown above that all things are common by nature, i.e., the right over other things was given to the human race by nature or God, the Author of nature. Now nature does not effect that this individual may have his right over this thing to the exclusion of the rest. Neither does she prohibit it, but permits it to be done provided a reasonable cause subsists, and, with this failing, reason persuades that nothing be changed. In the case of movable things, the cause of instituting property was that such things perish by use. Hence quarrels could scarcely fail to arise from common ownership, since this one would use a thing so that another having as much right in the same thing would not be able afterwards to use it. Moreover, in matters of the soil there was another reason, because things of the soil do not bear fruit "to a great extent" (which is sufficient in moral matters) unless stirred up by human labor and industry. Here again it was proper that fights be feared as a result of common ownership, since the industrious and hard-working men would be sorely tried that others whose labor was by no means equal bear off as much or even more of the fruits. Now both these reasons fail in the case of the sea. For by using, the sea itself is not at all impaired, and it needs no cultivation to bear fruit. Therefore the sea deservedly remained common; while fish, because they perish by use, become property, but in such a way as all things which belong to no one (*res nullius*), namely by occupation. For conflicts were being excellently met in the following manner. If any things could not remain common, they became the property of the first taker, both because the uncertainty of ownership could not otherwise be avoided and also because it was equitable that a premium be put upon diligence.

How explicitly the Roman jurists have said that the sea is the property of no one and that its use is common to all men, we have previously shown, in such a way as not to have done violence to them, but let him do violence who denies it. Yet Welwod, to charge this fault to me, in the last

---

155. Aristotle, *Nicomachean Ethics*, I. 3. 4 (1094b 24–25).

place adduces two responses, the first of Marcianus, the other of Papinian.[156] I doubt much whether he has seen them. For he says that Marcianus deals with a diverticulum of the sea, when nevertheless he openly deals with a diverticulum of a public river and not of the sea. The words are: "If anyone has been for many years the only one to fish in a diverticulum of a public river, he shall prohibit another from using the same right."[157] But this is to be taken, however, in accordance with what he asserts the same Papinian says, since the latter far from saying what Welwod claims, seems rather to support the contrary. "Prescription," he says, "of long custom is not usually granted for the acquisition of places which are public by the law of nations. This is the case, if anyone, after a building which he had placed on the shore had been completely destroyed and another's building afterwards had been constructed in the same place, should oppose the granting of an exception to the occupier, or if anyone, because he had been for many years the only one to fish in a diverticulum of a public river, should prohibit another from the same right."[158] I do not say that these passages can not be properly conciliated, if we say that Marcianus was speaking of him who had continued fishing, and Papinian of him who had abandoned fishing—which is not absurd to infer from the other example of the building destroyed on the shore. But meanwhile I can not marvel enough that, for the purpose of meeting the number of responses which we adduced in support of the community of the sea, two passages are produced, one of which does not properly pertain to the subject and the other upsets that for which it is adduced rather than confirms it.

More properly therefore would he have adduced the opinion of Paulus in *Digest*, XLVII. x. 14, for this is almost the only one in the entire *Corpus Juris* which seems to favor it. "Surely," says Paulus, "if property right over the sea belongs to anyone, the interdict *Uti possidetis* is competent to him, if he is prohibited from exercising his right, since this matter pertains to a private case, not to a public case, seeing that there is question of the enjoy-

156. Welwod, "Of the Community and Propriety of the Seas," pp. 72–73, above.
157. *Digest*, XLIV. 3. 7.
158. *Digest*, XLI. 3. 45.

ment of a right arising out of a private case, not out of a public case." But we have really said in the *Mare Liberum* that by these words of Paulus is understood a diverticulum of the sea,[159] just as Marcianus speaks of a diverticulum of a river. Welwod can not deny this, for in Chapter XXVI are his very words:

> Yea, nowadays, in rivers and in parts of the seas accrest to the possessions of men having grant and infeftment from the King, may fishing be forbidden; but no private man, without the grant of the prince, upon any pretense or allegation of long consuetude and prescription, may acquire the propriety of any such part of the sea so as to prohibit others to fish there also, for such prescriptions only pertain to princes.[160]

Welwod concedes here that no portion of the sea can be acquired by a private individual by way of possession. But Paulus is dealing with a private individual, upon Welwod's admission. It follows therefore that Paulus is not dealing with a portion of the sea. Therefore since nevertheless Paulus lays down that property right over the sea could belong to anyone, it remains that he is dealing not with the entire sea or with a portion of the sea, but with a diverticulum of the sea, which is improperly called the sea itself, just as the Lake of Asphalt is called the sea. That this is the opinion of Paulus is evident likewise from the response of Marcianus. For if in the case of a river, which is the property of the people, nothing can be acquired by way of possession except a diverticulum, much less will any of the sea, which is common to all, become property, except a diverticulum. Add that the chief reason impeding occupation, namely, because the sea can not be enclosed, does not cease except in the case of a diverticulum alone; and a diverticulum of the sea is very like the air shut up in a building, which it is not absurd for anyone to say becomes property.

To Welwod's query why that is not permitted to a prince which is permitted to a private individual and his broad praise of the prince's care in conserving the safety of the sea,[161] I shall reply that we deny nothing to a

159. Grotius, *The Free Sea*, p. 29, above.
160. Welwod, *Abridgement of All Sea-Lawes*, pp. 57–58.
161. Welwod, "Of the Community and Propriety of the Seas," p. 73, above.

prince which is granted to a private individual, but grant much to him which is not granted to a private individual. A prince therefore can make a diverticulum his own property. But a portion of the sea united to its entirety should not be concealed under the name of a diverticulum. For there is a great difference between these two. For just as a part of the entire river is within the bank, while a diverticulum is beyond the strict line of the bank, so a part of the sea is this side the shore, a diverticulum beyond. The word itself indicates this, for *divertere* is to depart from the way. The reason likewise is different. A part of the sea is united to the entire sea, a diverticulum is as it were torn away from it. A part of the sea is restrained by no limits, while a diverticulum is sea water obtruding upon and as it were enclosed in the land. A part of the sea exists by nature, a diverticulum more by art, as we have proved by the testimony of Columella, Varro, Pliny, Martial.[162] If a diverticulum becomes property, it takes nothing away from the sea, while if parts of the sea could become property, the entirety which consists only of its parts could also.[163] But we ought to remember that the question here is whether through the nature of things and the law of nations a certain thing could become property. Now in this question the name and majesty of a prince adds no weight, since he can change neither the nature of things nor the law of nations. A prince no more than a private individual can hold that which can not *per se* be held. And with regard to the law that dictum of Harmenopulus is true: "And the universal laws prevail over the king."[164] Nor does guardianship make anything for ownership; for the prince is the guardian also of other properties, much more of common property.

I had cited the Constitutions of Leo "On the diverticula ($\pi\rho\acute{o}\theta\nu\rho\alpha$)."[165] Welwod therefore asks whether he had less authority "than the rest of the Roman emperors."[166] Over their own subjects surely Justinian and Leo had the same right. But for us they have not the same authority, because it is evident that Justinian made use of the most learned assistants in com-

---

162. Grotius, *The Free Sea*, p. 28, above.
163. Compare Grotius, *De Jure Belli ac Pacis*, II. 3. 8.
164. Harmenopulus, *Epitome juris civilis*, I. 1. 39.
165. Leo, *Novellae*, CII, CIV.
166. Welwod, "Of the Community and Propriety of the Seas," p. 73, above.

piling the law, so that in the entire *Corpus* of Justinian law a wonderful sense of justice and consummate knowledge of the ancient law of the Quirites stands out. Therefore it has happened that many peoples have of their own accord accepted the Justinian laws, as the Romans of old the Rhodian laws. But never has that honor been given to the laws of Leo or the other emperors.

And yet in this question surely, just as the authority of Leo is not prejudicial to us, so we do not depend upon the authority of Justinian. In controversies of the law of nations, not the commands of a single prince, but the voices of many centuries, of many men, must be listened to. The Emperor Claudius willed marriages between uncles and their brothers' daughters to be legitimate (*justas*); yet no one has conceded this to be law. Nor indeed will the deed of Leo or that which was decreed by him make much for the present controversy. For Leo does not ascribe ownership of the sea to himself so that he may grant it to anyone he wishes in accordance with his judgment, but that he may proclaim what is of right. Even if therein he had decreed something new, he could not have done this as a result of the nature of the thing, but of that compliance which subjects owe their prince. For, as Ulpian says, although a servitude could not be imposed upon the sea, nevertheless persons could be obliged either to do or to permit something.[167]

Not even this, however, does Leo arrogate to himself, but he confirms by his own law what he thought was just and equitable *per se*. Whether he is deceived herein or not I do not argue. Certainly his meaning is clear.

> This law also (he says) which takes away the right of maritime estates from those from whose shores the sea is visible, and which moreover subjects their owner to action for damages if he prohibits those who desire from fishing there, seemed to us to decree injustice.

And afterwards:

> But for my part I see no reason why it should be done so.

Likewise:

---

167. *Digest*, VIII. 4. 13.

For just as it is of right, in places on land, that whoever may be the owner of a house, besides its use he possesses the vestibule and courtyard also, so we think it is in harmony with reason that this should obtain also in places on the sea.[168]

Nor does that which has been decreed put an end to our inquiry. From the Constitutions of the same Leo (LVII, CII, CIII, CIV), it is apparent that in the Thracian Bosphorus the owners of maritime estates were accustomed to erect certain barriers (*epochas*), that is, fences (*septa*), by which they enclosed in their estates some part of the sea to which they laid claim. If anyone else wished to fish here, it was doubtful whether he could be prohibited. The ancients had said no and had granted an action for damages to the one prohibited. Leo on the contrary thinks the right of prohibition is competent to the owners. It is in Leo's favor that that fencing is either occupation or something approximating occupation, and the little gate of the sea, thus limited by the barriers after the nature of a diverticulum and like a pier erected in the sea, seems to be in the class of things which can become property. On the other hand, it is in favor of the ancient jurists that the entire sea owes a common use to men, and that the right of a part should be the same as of the whole.[169] In this inquiry, if anyone prefers to follow the opinion of Leo rather than that of all the ancients, I shall not quarrel with him, provided however Leo's decree with regard to a little part enclosed be not extended, against the intention of Leo, to portions that are open and in fact indistinguishable from the sea.

Welwod says that I have made two concessions from which he promises himself victory. The first is with regard to the diverticulum; and to this we have already replied, indeed we had previously replied in the *Mare Liberum* itself. The other is this, which he says I wrote: "And if any of these could be prohibited, say for example, fishing, by which it can be said in a certain fashion that fish are exhaustible."[170] These words thus arranged have no sense. The entire sentence therefore should be described, which is as follows:

168. Leo, *Novellae,* LVI.
169. *Digest,* VI. 1. 76.
170. Welwod, "Of the Community and Propriety of the Seas," pp. 73–74, above.

Moreover, also he that should have authority over the sea could diminish nothing of the common use, as the people of Rome could hinder none from using all things in the shore of the empire of Rome which were permitted by the law of nations. And if it could forbid any of those things, to wit, fishing, whereby it may be said after a sort that fishes should be taken, yet they could not forbid navigation, whereby the sea loseth nothing.[171]

Who does not see that there is no concession here, but an argument is carried along which is frequent in law, that to him to whom something less is not permitted, much less is something greater permitted. Now it is less to prohibit fishing than navigation, because there are more reasons forbidding the prohibition of navigation than of fishing. A reason common to both is that the sea is open to all. There is added in the case of navigation the particular reason that through navigation nothing is taken away from the sea. And here is in point that passage I adduced from Cicero's *On Duties,* Book I,[172] which Welwod improperly ties up with fishing.

Moreover, that I have not conceded that fishing on the sea can be prohibited by anyone, is sufficiently apparent from the whole of Chapter V. If I had conceded it, Welwod would have undertaken this labor in vain. Indeed he who has properly taken the sequence and sense of my words, will easily see in that very passage what he takes as if conceded is in fact impugned. For I said that there was less injustice in the prohibition of fishing than of navigation, so that, since I had shown that the prohibition of fishing was illicit, it would on this account be more apparent how opposed the prohibition of navigation would be to every species of right.

But if anyone wishes to argue thus: since the fact that a thing is by nature communicable without any detriment is the reason why its use should not be prohibited, and this is wanting in the case of fishing, therefore fishing can be prohibited; whoever is not unskilled in logic will reply that the argument proceeds from the removal of the cause to the removal of the effect only if beyond that cause other sufficient causes can not be given. But here are many other sufficient causes which forbid the prohibition of

171. Grotius, *The Free Sea,* p. 37, above.
172. Cicero, *De officiis,* I. 16. 8.

fishing, as this, that the sea, since it is not occupable, can become the property of no one; moreover, because of the fact that it is no one's property, its fruits may be gathered by anyone, as can be shown from the example of herbs and other things growing in lands newly discovered. Secondly, although there may be no other causes, nevertheless the law of nations itself, whether it arises from a secret instinct of nature or from the primitive custom of the human race, would be sufficient to introduce the obligation.[173]

Welwod complains that great injuries to the British are inflicted by the Batavian fishermen.[174] How then? Because they catch fish indeed? But he is not to be considered as inflicting an injury who makes use of his own right.[175] If the Batavians prohibited the British from fishing, they would be doing them injury. Now why unless they are using a common thing in common. If the British please, they can not only fish beside the Batavians, but also outstrip the Batavians, since they themselves are nearer the sea where fish are plentiful. But if they weary of the great labor, weary of the expense which with the greatest frugality nevertheless frequently eats up all the profit, why begrudge the fact that what is neglected by themselves is taken by their neighbors? Add now the fact that if he who fishes in the sea is to be considered as inflicting injury upon another, because the other can not fish in the same place and at the same time, to this example add also that he who navigates can be considered as injuring another, because the two can not navigate at the same time in the same place. But if Welwod intended this, namely, that those fish are dispersed and scattered which are not caught, this, apart from the fact that we do not believe it true, certainly should be attributed to navigation, not to fishing; so that he who wishes to prohibit this, should prohibit navigation up to the shore. But it is well known in law that those things which happen on account of the destination "and *per accidens*" are never imputed to those using their own right.[176]

We have shown that we conceded nothing to Welwod which pertains

---

173. Compare Grotius, *De Jure Belli ac Pacis,* II. 3. 11–12.
174. Welwod, "Of the Community and Propriety of the Seas," p. 74, above.
175. *Digest,* XXXIX. 2. 24, § 12; *Digest,* L. 7. 151.
176. *Digest,* XXXIX. 3. 1, § 12; *Digest,* XXXIX. 3. 2, § 9.

to claiming the sea or the right of fishing in one's own right. Let us see whether I can not rather draw forth some weapons for myself out of his armory.

This is the first one given by Welwod, namely, that private individuals, unless they have received it from a prince, can not acquire for themselves any portion of the sea or the right of prohibiting fishing, because a right of this kind of prescriptions belongs to the prince alone. His words are in Chapter XXVI and from them we may argue as follows.[177] Whatever belongs to a prince, if it is alienable, can be sought also by a private individual by prescription. But a portion of the sea and the right of prohibiting fishing can not be sought by a private individual by prescription, nor does this happen because they are not susceptible of being conceded. It follows therefore that they do not belong to the prince. The major proposition is proved from the fact that by the law of nations, so far as ownership of property is concerned, there is no distinction between prince and private individual, while it is a most certain rule of civil law that whatever can be acquired by privilege or concession can be acquired by a possession of time exceeding memory. The assumption is from Welwod's words. He confesses that it is not inalienable or unsusceptible of being conceded when he posits that such a right can be sought through the beneficence of a prince, and yet denies that it can be acquired by prescription.

Again it will be permissible to argue in another way as follows. Whatever belongs to the people can be acquired by a private individual by a possession exceeding memory. But the sea can not be acquired by a private individual by such a possession. Therefore it does not belong to the people. The assumption here is from Welwod's words. But the major proposition can be proved "by induction." And there is excellent testimony to this fact in *Code*, XI. 42. 4, if you compare *Digest*, XXXIX. 3. 18. § 1, and *Digest*, XLIII. 20. 20. § 42.

Moreover, from this statement, that this prescription, whereby a portion of the sea or the right of fishing is acquired, belongs to the prince alone, another argument is at hand for him as follows. No one can obtain

---

177. Welwod, *Abridgement of All Sea-Lawes*, p. 57.

by prescription what is his before, because what is mine can not become more mine. But the prince is here said to obtain by prescription a portion of the sea or the right of fishing. Therefore it is not his before prescription. If it is not his before, then such things do not belong to the prince by any common law nor can they be acquired by occupation. For there is no need to do anything to acquire that which belongs to us *ipso jure,* and occupation is completed in a single act, whereas prescription requires a continued act and indeed of very long duration.

Therefore all those arguments of Welwod fail, which either aim to make the prince owner of the sea *ipso jure* or claim that from the beginning the sea was occupied no less than the lands. Finally, let it be added that, when Welwod denies that a portion of the sea or the right of prohibiting fishing can be acquired by private individuals apart from the beneficence of the prince, the law of the *Digest,* XLVII. 10. 14, does not help him, since there is question there of that right which arises from a private case, not from a public case. Yet this is the one place in all the law, which has led into error all those who hitherto have departed from the opinion we defended.

The second argument which Welwod has given is that navigation can not be prohibited by anyone whomsoever in any part of the sea.[178] Since this is quite true, it can arise only from such a law of nations as obliges all nations. Now who believes that such a principle of the greatest importance has been overlooked by the ancient jurists who so diligently pursued all of the law of nations? But he will find no mention of it save in those words which assert that the sea is owned by no one or that its use is common to all men. Whence I infer that these very axioms, that the sea is owned by no one and its use is common to all men, are not of that civil law which by imitation has become common to many peoples and which is incorrectly called law of nations, but of the law of nations properly so-called, which obliges nations to nations. For from the effect the cause is recognized. But that it is illicit to prohibit navigation comes from those axioms. Hence also I infer that in those axioms the words "no one" and "all" are to be understood absolutely universally and not of the citizens of one peo-

178. Welwod, "Of the Community and Propriety of the Seas," p. 65, above.

ple, because navigation can not be prohibited not only to citizens, but neither also to foreigners. Universal effects can not proceed from a particular cause.

Upon the supposition that those axioms are of the real law of nations and are to be taken universally, it will easily be apparent that fishing likewise is open to all without distinction. For fishing likewise is using the sea, and the fruits of what belongs to no one become the property of the occupier. And therefore Ulpian and Marcianus by denying ownership and positing the common use of the sea itself are arguing freedom of fishing.[179] The force of this consequence led Angelus and those who have the same hallucination with him to assert that, because as a result of a misinterpretation of a response of Paulus they had decided that fishing on the sea could be prohibited, therefore a part of the sea could become the property of someone. But on this hypothesis they could extend the argument so as not to be afraid to assert that navigation can likewise be prohibited. How absurd and injurious this is Welwod sees. He should be asked therefore to permit the sources of his errors to be closed up.

The third argument accepted by me as a gift from Welwod is as follows: " 'The sea can not become the property of anyone because nature bids it be common.' . . . To whom I could also assent concerning the great, huge, and main body of the sea."[180] And afterwards: "I think that the sea should be proclaimed free, I mean that part of the main sea or great Ocean, which is far removed from bounds."[181] Here again I shall repeat that, since this is quite true and of great moment, it has not been overlooked by the ancient jurists. But nowhere have they handed this down unless in the passages cited by us, wherein it is proclaimed that the sea has come into the ownership of no one and by the law of nations its use is common to all men. Hence it is clear again, as I have just said, that in those passages the question is of the true and proper law of nations and those propositions are to be understood absolutely universally. Now these same jurists simply mention the sea and make no distinction whether it is nearer or farther from

---

179. Compare Grotius, *De Jure Belli ac Pacis,* II. 2. 11–13.
180. Welwod, "Of the Community and Propriety of the Seas," p. 72, above.
181. Ibid., p. 74, above.

the land whether it is vast or not vast. Whence therefore that distinction for us? Why, that distinction can not only not be proved, but it is even easily refuted. For quantity and situs do not make different species of substances. Moreover how can the law of one species be different, and indeed from the law of nations which especially is equal and universal?

Add the fact that Welwod claims that certain parts, not of the Mediterranean Sea but of the ocean, become property, and everything which he brings forward to defend the ownership of those parts can be applied less properly to other vaster parts of the ocean. For if in those parts with which Welwod is concerned are islands, rocks, shallows, you may find them also in the Atlantic Ocean. If those parts have shores, so has the Atlantic Ocean. And what reason operates, if the sea can be occupied up to one hundred miles, to prevent it being occupied up to 150, thence to 200 and so on? If water is property up to the 100th mile, why can not the water which is immediately contiguous to the property be equally property? These are the "impasses" ($\grave{\alpha}\pi o\rho\iota\alpha\varsigma$) to which you must come, once you have departed from the truth. Indeed if Welwod's statement is correct, that, although the parts of the sea are not limited, nevertheless the entire body of the sea is limited and therefore occupable, it will follow that the entire Ocean can more easily become property than the individual parts, since they cohere to the Ocean and therefore are not bound by certain limits.[182]

And so far indeed we have defended, sufficiently, I think, the opinion already proposed by us concerning the community of the sea and the freedom of fishing. Purposely have we refrained from treating of the dominion (*imperium*) and jurisdiction of the sea, because that question has no connection with ownership (*dominium*) and the right of fishing and consequently is improperly confused by Welwod with this controversy of ours. Therefore although I could have passed over the treatment of this matter, nevertheless, in order that the reader may find nothing lacking, I shall say what I think: that to be done properly, I think we should have regard not so much for the interpreters, who lived a few centuries back and who often

---

182. Compare Grotius, *De Jure Belli ac Pacis*, II. 3. 8, 10.

disagree from others and from each other, as for the ancient authorities and the very principles and rules of the law themselves.

Wherefore lest different matters be falsely confused, I think a distinction should be made between that jurisdiction which is competent to each in common and that which is competent to each one properly speaking. All peoples or their princes in common can punish pirates and others, who commit delicts on the sea against the law of nations. For even supposing a land that has been occupied by no people, there will be the same right against brigands lurking there. Now jurisdiction, which is competent to each one in his own right is directed toward either a person or a thing or place. A jurisdiction over a person is competent without taking account of the place. For a prince can forbid his subjects even not to do such and such a thing outside his territory, and in this way those who send ambassadors command the ambassadors though they act at a distance. In turn jurisdiction can be directed toward a place without taking account of the person. So laws are decreed for transient visitors by him who has dominion over the soil through which the passage is made. Again jurisdiction over a person results either from the institution of the state itself, as that of the supreme power over subjects, or from agreement over allies. Consequently not only can the prince make law for the maritime actions of his subjects, judge these acts, even impose tribute, but also do this for his allies, if this has been agreed to by treaty. For, as we have said following Ulpian,[183] even when a thing can not be subject, nevertheless persons can be put under obligation by convention. Nor do I deny that what can be induced by treaty can be induced by tacit consent, that is, by custom, provided the custom be not extended beyond those who by long sufferance can be considered to have bestowed their assent.

So far I do not oppose those who maintain some jurisdiction over the sea. But if anyone insists further that over the sea no less than over ground that has been occupied there is also a certain local or real jurisdiction, I should very much like to learn by what reasons or testimony of the ancients it can be proved. I have read no reasons for this opinion. Indeed I

183. *Digest,* VIII. 4. 13.

think there are not lacking strong reasons for the contrary view, if one properly considered that territories arose from the occupation of peoples, just as private ownerships from the occupation of private individuals. The ancient authorities, especially the jurists whom this treatise properly concerns, have nowhere, if I mistake not, handed this down. There are Rhodian laws, there are Attic laws, there are Roman laws on maritime matters, but all these are directed toward subjects. Therefore there is no reason why we should refer them to dominion of place, since, as we have just said, subjects are wont to be commanded even when acting in foreign territory, how much more when they are in that place over which the jurisdiction of all peoples is common. But I do not find laws or tributes imposed upon foreigners when acting on the sea.

Some perhaps may be moved by the reply of Celsus (for beyond this I see nothing which can be adduced in point) when he says that the shores are among those places over which the Roman people have dominion, and he even calls the shores the Roman people's. But when he forthwith notes that the use of the sea, as of the air, is common to all men, it seems manifest that he makes a distinction in this matter between the sea and the shores.[184] We have discussed above what could be understood by the term "shore" in that passage. Certainly no one could deny that the shore is more easily occupied than the sea, being permanent in its very nature. Plutarch, Velleius and others relate that pirates on the sea were captured by Gaius Julius Caesar while still a private citizen and that when the proconsul neglected to punish them, Caesar sailed back on the sea and there the pirates were crucified by him. Caesar would no more have dared this on the sea than in the province, indeed would have committed *lese majesty*, if the sea had been as much the territory of the Roman people as the province itself. Such is my view, but if any one should point out a better, I shall gladly yield mine.

But, as I began to say, our controversy is over the ownership of the sea and the prohibition of fishing. Now foreign to this is the question of jurisdiction. For first, ownership is separate from dominion (*imperium*),

---

184. *Digest,* XLIII. 8. 3; *Digest,* XLIII. 8. 3, § 1.

consequently law (*jus*) is declared with regard to other matters; secondly, the authority of declaring the law or of exercising dominion is restrained by the law of nations. The prince exercises dominion and declares the law not with regard to human matters only, but also with regard to divine matters, but he can not order what has been forbidden by God or forbid what has been ordered by God. The supreme power has the judgment over civil laws and guardianship and protection over divine law, natural law and the law of nations. Therefore even if a prince has real jurisdiction over the sea and indeed the Ocean, this would not have anything to do with his claiming ownership of the sea, but with his guarding its community; not with his prohibiting fishing to any man, but with defending the freedom of fishing. Nor is anything else meant by those more recent writers, whom Welwod adduces to prove that territory extends into the sea also.[185]

Although in all this dissertation I have trod in the footprints of the old writers, almost omitting the more recent masters, who through too much or too little time or zeal for a cause undertaken have wandered from the true reason of law, yet that it may be evident that I am defending not only my own commentary but also the received opinion of the greater and better part, I shall add here what others have written on the same subject, and shall summon as the judge of this controversy like a Senate one of the most learned men from Italy, Germany, France, Britain and Spain.

Rest lacking.

185. Compare Grotius, *De Jure Belli ac Pacis,* II. 3. 13–15.

BIBLIOGRAPHY

Works of Hugo Grotius

PUBLISHED WORKS

Grotius, Hugo. *Briefwisseling van Hugo Grotius.* Edited by P. C. Molhuysen, B. L. Meulenbroek, and H. J. M. Nellen. 17 vols. The Hague: M. Nijhoff, 1928–2001.

Grotius, Hugo. *De Jure Belli ac Pacis Libri Tres.* Edited by Francis W. Kelsey. 2 vols. Oxford: Clarendon Press, 1925.

Grotius, Hugo. *De Jure Praedae Commentarius.* Edited by H. G. Hamaker. The Hague, 1868.

Grotius, Hugo. *De Jure Praedae Commentarius.* I: *Commentary on the Law of Prize and Booty.* Translated by Gwladys L. Williams and Walter H. Zeydel. II: *The Collotype Reproduction of the Original Manuscript of 1604 in the Handwriting of Grotius.* 2 vols. Oxford: Clarendon Press, 1950.

Grotius, Hugo. "Defensio capitis quinti Maris Liberi oppugnati a Guilielmo Welwodo . . . capite XXVII ejus libri . . . cui titulum fecit Compendium Legum Maritimarum." In *Mare Clausum: Bijdrage tot de Geschiedenis der Rivaliteit van Engeland en Nederland in de Zeventiende Eeuw,* by Samuel Muller, 331–61. Amsterdam: F. Muller, 1872.

Grotius, Hugo. "Defense of Chapter V of the *Mare Liberum.*" In "Some Less Known Works of Hugo Grotius," translated by Herbert F. Wright. *Bibliotheca Visseriana* 7 (1928): 154–205.

Grotius, Hugo. *Mare Liberum, sive De Jure quod Batavis competit ad Indicana commercio.* Leiden, 1609.

Grotius, Hugo. *Mare Liberum, sive De Jure quod Batavis competit ad Indicana commercio.* New York: Carnegie Endowment for International Peace, 1952.

Grotius, Hugo. *The Freedom of the Seas.* Translated by Ralph Van Deman Magoffin. New York: Oxford University Press, American Branch, 1916.

Grotius, Hugo. *Von der Freiheit des Meeres.* Edited and translated by Richard Boschan. Leipzig: F. Meiner, 1919.

MANUSCRIPT

Grotius, Hugo. "The Free Sea." Translated by Richard Hakluyt. MS Petyt 529. Inner Temple Library, London.

Other Works Referred to in the Text and Notes

All classical references have been verified in the standard editions and translations available in the Loeb Classical Library.

Accursius. *Glossa in Digestum novum.* Venice, 1487.

Alciati, Andrea. *Opera Omnia.* Frankfurt, 1617.

Alsop, J. D. "William Welwood, Anne of Denmark and the Sovereignty of the Sea." *Scottish Historical Review* 49 (1980): 171–74.

Ambrose. *De Nabuthe.* In *Patrologia Latina,* ed. Migne, XIV.

———. *De officiis ministrorum.* In *Patrologia Latina,* ed. Migne, XVI.

———. *Hexaemeron.* In *Patrologia Latina,* ed. Migne, XIV.

Angelus de Ubaldis [Angelo degli Ubaldi]. *Consilia.* Frankfurt, 1575.

———. *In Digestum vetus.* Lyons, 1561.

———. *Super I–IX Codicis.* Milan, 1487.

Aquinas, Thomas. *Secunda secundae Sancti Thomae . . . domini Thomae de Vio, Caietani . . . commentaribus adornata.* Lyon, 1540.

Arthus, Gotthard. *Dialogues in the English and Malaiane Languages.* Translated by Augustine Spalding. London, 1614.

Augustine. *De civitate Dei.* 7 vols. Cambridge, Mass.: Harvard University Press, 1957–72.

———. *Questionum in Heptateuchum.* In *Patrologia Latina,* ed. Migne, XXXIV.

Avienus, Rufius Festus. *Arati Phaenomena.* Edited by Jean Soubiran. Paris: Les Belles Lettres, 1981.

Ayala, Balthazar. *De jure et officiis bellicis et disciplina militari libri III.* Edited by John Westlake. Washington, D.C.: Carnegie Institution of Washington, 1912.

Balbus, Joannes Franciscus [Giovanni Francesco Balbi]. *De praescriptionibus.* Cologne, 1573.

Baldus de Ubaldis [Baldo degli Ubaldi]. *Consiliorum.* 5 vols. Venice, 1608–9.

———. *Super Digesto veteri.* 2 vols. Lyons, 1535.

———. *Super Feudis.* Lyons, 1566.

Bartolus of Sassoferrato. *Opera omnia.* Venice, 1596.

———. *Tyberiadis . . . tractatus de fluminibus tripertitus.* Bologna, 1576.

Bernard of Clairvaux. *De consideratione.* In *Patrologia Latina,* ed. Migne, CLXXXII.

Borschberg, Peter. "The Seizure of the *Sta. Catarina* Revisited: The Portuguese Empire in Asia, VOC Politics and the Origins of the Dutch-Johor Alliance (1602–ca. 1616)." *Journal of Southeast Asian Studies* 33 (2002): 31–62.

Calendar of State Papers, Colonial Series. Edited by W. Nöel Sainsbury, et al. 40 vols. London: Great Britain Public Record Office, 1860–1926.

Cassiodorus, Flavius Magnus Aurelius. *Variae. Monumenta Germaniae Historica,* XII. Berlin: Weidmann, 1961.

Castrensis, Paulus [Paul de Castro]. *In primam Codicis partem commentaria.* 2 vols. Venice, 1582.

———. *In primam Digesti veteris partem commentaria.* 2 vols. Venice, 1582.

Castro, Alfonso de. *De potestate legis poenalis.* Lyon, 1566.

Clark, G. N., and van Eysinga, W. J. M. *The Colonial Conferences Between England and the Netherlands in 1613 and 1615, Bibliotheca Visseriana* 15 (1940).

Clement of Alexandria. *Stromata.* In *Ante-Nicene Fathers,* II, edited by Alexander Roberts and James Donaldson. 24 vols. Edinburgh, 1867–72.

Connan, François de. *Commentarium Juris civilis libri decem.* Hanau, 1609.

Corpus juris canonici, 2 ed. Edited by Emil Friedberg. Leipzig, 1879–81.

Covarruvias y Leyva, Diego de. *Opera omnia.* 2 vols. Venice, 1614.

Cowell, John. *Institutiones juris Anglicani ad methodam Institutionem imperialium compositae et digestae.* Cambridge, 1605.

Cujas, Jacques. *Opera omnia.* 6 vols. Lyon, 1606.

Documentos remettidos da India, ou Livros das monções. Edited by Raymundo Antonio de Bulhão Pato, et al. 10 vols. Lisbon: Royal Academy of Sciences, 1880–1982.

Doneau, Hugues. *Commentariorum de Jure civili libri viginti octo.* 5 vols. Frankfurt, 1595–97.

Douaren, François. *Omnia . . . opera.* Frankfurt, 1607.

Faber, Jean. *Super Institutionibus.* Lyon, 1557.

Fachineus, Andreus [Andrea Faccini]. *Controversiarum juris libri tredecim.* 2 vols. Cologne, 1626.

Felinus [Felino Maria Sandeo]. *Commentariorum in Decretalium libros V.* 3 vols. Venice, 1564.

Feudorum libri duo in Juris Civilis. Lyons, 1569.

Freitas, Justo Seraphim de. *De justo imperio Lusitanorum Asiatico.* Valladolid, 1625.

Fulton, Thomas Wemyss. *The Sovereignty of the Sea.* London: W. Blackwood, 1911.

Gentili, Alberico. *De jure belli libri tres.* Edited by C. Phillipson. 2 vols. Oxford: Clarendon Press, 1933.

[Glossators.] *Corpus glossatorum juris civilis.* General editor, Mario Viora. 11 vols. Turin: Ex Officina Erasmiana, 1966–73.

Guicciardini, Francesco. *Historia d'Italia.* Edited by Giovanni Rosini. 6 vols. Milan, 1850.

Haakonssen, Knud. "Hugo Grotius and the History of Political Thought." *Political Theory* 13 (1985): 239–65.

Hakluyt, Richard. *The Original Writings and Correspondence of the Two Richard Hakluyts.* Edited by E. G. R. Taylor. 2 vols. London: Hakluyt Society, 1935.

Harmenopulus, Constantinus. *Epitome juris civilis quae legum prochiron et hexabiblos inscribitur.* Paris, 1540.

Harrison, John, and Laslett, Peter. *The Library of John Locke.* Oxford: Oxford University Press, 1965.

Heinrich von Gorkum. *De bello justo.* In *Tractatus consultatorii,* fols. 50–57. Cologne, 1503.

Justinian. *Corpus juris civilis [The Civil Law].* Edited by S. P. Scott. 17 vols. Cincinnati: The Central Trust Company, 1932.

Locke, John. *Two Treatises of Government.* Edited by Peter Laslett. Cambridge: Cambridge University Press, 1988.

Mainus, Jason [Giasone del Maino]. *In primam Digesti veteris.* 2 vols. Venice, 1589.

Nazianzen, Gregory. "Panegyric on Basil." In *The Nicene and Post-Nicene Fathers,* VII, edited by Philip Schaff and Henry Wace. 14 vols. New York: Scribner and Sons, 1890–1900.

Nonius Marcellus. *De compendiosa doctrina libros XX.* Edited by W. M. Lindsay. 3 vols. Leipzig: B. G. Teubner, 1903.

Osório, Jerónimo. *De rebus Emmanuelis, Lusitania regis.* Cologne, 1547.

Panormitanus [Niccoló de' Tudeschi]. *Commentaria ad tertium libros decretalium.* 2 vols. Turin, 1577.

Parks, George Bruner. *Richard Hakluyt and the English Voyages.* New York: American Geographical Society, 1928.

Patrologiae cursus completus . . . series Latina. Edited by Jacques-Paul Migne. 221 vols. Paris, 1844–64.

Placentinus, Petrus. *In Summam Institutionum.* Lyon, 1536.

Quinn, D. B., ed. *The Hakluyt Handbook.* 2 vols. London: Hakluyt Society, 1974.

Reusch, F. H. *Der Index der verbotenen Bücher.* 2 vols. Bonn: M. Cohen and Son, 1883–85.

Rogers, F. M. "Hakluyt as Translator." In *The Hakluyt Handbook,* edited by D. B. Quinn, I, 37–47.

Selden, John. *Mare Clausum seu De dominio maris.* London, 1635.

Siete Partidas, Las. Translated by S. P. Scott and edited by Robert I. Burns. 5 vols. Philadelphia: University of Pennsylvania Press, 2001.

Sigonio, Carlo. *Opera omnia.* 6 vols. Milan, 1732–37.

Solórzano Pereira, Juan. *De Indiarum jure.* 2 vols. Madrid, 1629.

Stobaeus. *Florilegium.* Edited by Thomas Gainsford. 4 vols. Oxford, 1822.

Suárez, Rodericus [Roderigo Juárez]. *Consilia duo . . . de usu maris.* Benvenuto Stracca, *Tractatus de mercatura seu de mercatore,* 850–68. Cologne, 1576.

Sylvester Prierias [Silvestro Mazzolini da Priero]. *Summa Silvestrina.* 2 vols. Lyons, 1524.

Theophilus. *Paraphrasis . . . in Juris civilis institutiones.* Geneva, 1610.

Torquemada, Juan de. *Summa de ecclesia.* Rome, 1489.

Tuck, Richard. *Philosophy and Government, 1572–1651.* Cambridge: Cambridge University Press, 1993.

———. *The Rights of War and Peace: Political Thought and the International Order from Grotius to Kant.* Oxford: Oxford University Press, 1999.

Van Ittersum, Martine. "Profit and Principle: Hugo Grotius, Natural Rights Theories and the Rise of Dutch Power in the East Indies, 1595–1615." Ph.D. dissertation, Harvard University, 2002.

Vázquez de Menchaca, Fernando. *Controversiarum illustrium . . . libri tres.* Frankfurt, 1572.

———. *De successione . . . resolutione.* Salamanca, 1559.

Vitoria, Francisco de. *Political Writings.* Edited by Anthony Pagden and Jeremy Lawrance. Cambridge: Cambridge University Press, 1991.

Welwod, William. *An Abridgement of All Sea-Lawes.* London, 1613.

———. *De dominio maris.* London, 1615.

———. *The Sea Law of Scotland.* Edinburgh, 1590.

INDEX

Paulus (jurist): on access to sea, 117–
18; on access to shore, 90; on natural possession, 107; on occupation,
108, 110; on possession, 109, 113;
on possession of sea, 70; on public
use, 103; on use of sea, 29, 42, 126
peace: in maintenance of trade, 57–
60; types of, 57
Philip (archduke of Flanders), 114
Philip III (king of Spain), 61–62
pirates, punishment of, 128, 129
Placentinus, on use of sea, 30, 69
Plautius (jurist), 103
Plautus, common use in, 26, 72,
84
Pliny the Elder: on trade, 50; on voyages of discovery, 35
Pliny the Younger, on divine justice,
10
Plutarch, 15
Pomponius, Sextus: on access to
shore, 101, 102; on common use,
27, 68; on losses, 74; on public
use, 103; on use of sea, 97; on warfare, 60
ports, public use of, 91, 114
Portugal: access to East Indies, xv;
dominium over seas, xvii, 32, 33,
34; in East Indies market, xii; garrisons in Indies, 37; hindrance of
navigation, 12; *imperium* over East
Indies, 13–20; prescription of
trade, 53–56; prescriptions of, 39–
49; renewal of navigation, 35–36;
voyages of exploration, 34, 48; war
crimes of, xiv; wealth of, 36
Portuguese, impieties of, 19–20
possessio (physical seizure), xiii; *dominium* through, xvi
possession: by act of mind, 113–14; of
common property, 33–35; community of, 86, 116; and exploration,

34; and finding, 14; following occupation, 110; of immovables, 110;
limitations on, 107–8, 109; of
movables, 109, 116; natural, 107–8,
109; through necessity, xix; in Old
Testament, 19; and ownership,
112–13; *per aliud,* 110; and right of
navigation, 20–38; in Roman law,
109, 113; in Scripture, 19; succession of parts in, 115; territorial *versus* maritime, xvi, xvii, xix;
through warfare, 17. *See also dominium*
postliminium, right of, 108
praetors, authority of, 101, 102, 103,
104
prescription: in civil law, 39, 45; in
common use, 41–42, 45; in commonwealths, 41; and custom, 42;
exceptions to, 41; of fishing rights,
40, 46, 124, 125; in law of nations,
43, 45; in natural law, 45; of navigation, 39–49; *versus* occupation,
125; of princes, 124; of public
property, 39–43, 48; of rights, 124–
25; on rivers, 46, 47; of time out of
mind, 41–42, 47–48, 54; of trade,
53–54
princes: authority of, 120; authority
over property, 119; dominion of,
130; laws of, 6–8, 99–100; maritime legislation of, 128; prescriptions of, 124; right over sea, 38,
118–19; role in civil law, 100
prizes: universal law of, 77; in warfare, xiii
proofs, Aristotle on, 115-16
property: authority of princes over,
119; Cicero on, 24, 82, 85; division
of, 93; Grotius's theory of, xix; immovable, 81; invention of, 22; in
law of nations, 124; modern theo-

This book is set in Adobe Garamond, a modern adaptation by Robert Slimbach of the typeface originally cut around 1540 by the French typographer and printer Claude Garamond. The Garamond face, with its small lowercase height and restrained contrast between thick and thin strokes, is a classic "old-style" face and has long been one of the most influential and widely used typefaces.

Printed on paper that is acid-free and meets the requirements of the American National Standard for Permanence of Paper for Printed Library Materials, z39.48-1992. ⊗

Book design by Louise OFarrell
Gainesville, Florida
Typography by Impressions Book and Journal Services, Inc.
Madison, Wisconsin
Printed and bound by Worzalla Publishing Company
Stevens Point, Wisconsin